Science Panorama 8

Physics

Series Editor
Versha Jayaswal

Collins

Science Panorama 8

Physics

Series Editor

Versha Jayaswal

Preface

Science Panorama is a series of books for Classes 1 to 8, which includes 3 books each for Physics, Chemistry and Biology for middle school. The middle school series has been updated based on the **new syllabus** prescribed by the **Council for the Indian School Certificate Examinations**. In line with the new syllabus, a thematic, coherent and structured approach has been followed and all the new topics suggested in the syllabus have been included. Chapter-wise worksheets have also been provided to effectively integrate subject knowledge and life skills for overall development.

This updated edition also emphasizes on developing scientific skills such as observation, investigation, analysis, research and other inferential skills. It focuses on concepts as well as their application in real life. Sufficient examples from everyday life have been provided to help learners understand the concepts using age-appropriate language. Colourful illustrations and well-labelled diagrams have been included to engage learners and aid their understanding.

Some Key Features

Science in Context: Additional information on the topic being taught

Do You Know? Interesting facts related to the given topic

Challenge Yourself: Questions testing students' ability to reason and extrapolate

Activities: Individual/collaborative activities to hone experimental and deduction skills

Know the Scientist: Famous scientists and their contribution to the topic at hand

Solved Problems: Numerical problems with solutions

Revision Zone: In-text questions for assessing progress during the course of learning

Keywords: Important words from the chapter along with their definitions

In a Nutshell: Summary for quick recapitulation

Exercise: Variety of questions given at the end of each chapter

Subject Integration Worksheets: To effectively integrate knowledge across subjects

Life Skills Worksheets: To create awareness, empathy and a positive attitude towards self and others

Assessment papers: Two assessment papers at the end of the book for effective evaluation

Things to Remember: Summary of all important formulas, equations and units (at the end of each book)

We would like to take this opportunity to thank all the teachers who reviewed the books and provided their valuable feedback which helped in improving the quality of the content.

Any suggestions or constructive criticism from the users are welcome. We shall try to incorporate those in the future editions.

Authors

Key Features

Science in Context

Compared to car tyres, a tractor's tyres are wide and have deep treads. The deep treads help the tyres to move through slippery mud and dirt that do not provide any friction. The larger width of the tyres provides enough surface to compensate the pressure from the weight of the tractor.

Science in Context

Additional information on the topic being taught

Do You Know?

Light from the sun takes about 8 minutes 20 seconds to reach Earth. How does the sunlight reach Earth in a few minutes even though the sun is 150 million km away from Earth? This is because light travels at the speed of 3×10^8 m/s.

Do You know?

Interesting facts related to the given topic

Challenge Yourself

You might have seen people hula hooping; spinning and balancing the hoops around them. Find out the types of motions involved in hula hooping.

Challenge Yourself

Questions testing students' ability to reason and extrapolate

Solved Problems

Numerical problems with solutions

Solved Problems

1. Calculate the density of a substance wh

   Solution:

   Mass = 500 g, volume = 40 cm^3

   Density = $\frac{\text{mass}}{\text{volume}} = \frac{500}{40}$ = 12.5 g/c

2. Calculate the mass of a spherical object

   Solution:

   Radius (r) = 3 cm, density = 2 g/cm^3

   First, we need to find the volume o

   of the spheric

Know the Scientist

Famous scientists and their contribution to the topic at hand

...bility ...d of ..., play, ...es also ...non-living

...cause the

...hen we ...nergy

Know the Scientist

The SI unit of energy and work, joule, is named in the honour of the English scientist, **James Prescott Joule**. He was the first to study the nature of heat and its relationship with mechanical energy, which eventually led to the law of conservation of energy.

Activity

Activities to hone experimental skills

...water = 1000 kg...

...bstance = relative density of the subs...

...e, density of iron = 7.87 × 1000 kg/m³ = 7870 kg/m...

...ng and Sinking

...bject will float or sink depending on its density and the density o... ...e following activity will help us understand floating and sinking.

Activity 3

Aim: To understand floating and sinking with respect to density

Materials required: Two beakers, water, kerosene, wooden block, a nail

Procedure:

Case 1:

Fill the two beakers with water. Place the wooden block in one beaker and the nail in the other beaker. Observe what happens in both the beakers.

Case 2:

...ll one beaker with water and one with kerosene. Place the ...den block first in water and then in kerosene. Observe ...appens to the block when placed in both the beakers.

...ion and Conclusion:

...it is less dense than water. Th...

Exercise

Variety of questions given at the end of each chapter

...e cube v. exp... of liqu...

5 Define the following.

a. Heat b. Melting poi...
c. Freezing point d. Temperature
e. Conductors f. Insulators

6 Differentiate between the following.

a. Inflammable and non-flammable materials
b. Conduction and convection
c. Clinical thermometer and labor... thermometer
... Melting point and freezin...
... ...s scale and F...

Remember

Highlighting/recalling the key points of the concept

Remember

Work is done on an object when:

- we lift it up
- we lower it
- we speed it up
- we slow it down

...f the object. Then,

Worksheet

Thematic worksheets on integration of knowledge across subjects and Life Skills

Worksheet

A Subject Integration

Depict the movement of the particles for the given change of states o...

1. Boiling
2. Evaporation
3. Freezing

Contents

Matter

1

Introduction

What I shall learn

- Properties of matter
- Kinetic theory of matter
- Arrangement of molecules in three states of matter
- Change of state in matter

We are surrounded by different objects, for example, water, air and trees. Every object around us is made up of matter. The air we breathe and the water we drink are also matter. So, let us understand what actually is matter?

Anything that has mass and occupies space is called **matter**. All matter is particulate in nature. This means that matter is made up of tiny particles. These particles are called atoms. Matter exists in three different states—solid, liquid and gas. For example,

- pencil is a solid • water is a liquid • air is a gas

How do you think we arrived at this conclusion? This is because each state of matter has different physical properties. Let us learn more about matter in this chapter.

Properties of the Three States of Matter

The properties of solids, liquids and gases are summarized in Table 1.1.

Table 1.1 Properties of the three states of matter

Solids	Liquids	Gases
Have a fixed shape, size and volume	Do not have a fixed shape but have a fixed volume	Do not have a fixed shape and volume
Not easily compressible	More compressible compared to solids	Easily compressible
Do not flow easily	Flow easily from higher level to lower level	Can flow in all directions easily

Remember

An atom is made up of subatomic particles called protons, neutrons and electrons. Protons and neutrons form the nucleus of the atom, while electrons revolve around the nucleus in orbits.

Composition of Matter

Atoms are the basic building blocks of matter. They are extremely small in size and can be seen only with the help of very powerful microscopes. All atoms are not of the same type. They differ from each other with respect to the number of subatomic particles (i.e., protons, neutrons and electrons) they have. That is, the property of an atom is determined by the number of protons, neutrons and electrons it is made up of.

When all the atoms that make up a substance are of the same type, then the substance is called an **element**. Thus, an element represents one type of atoms. There are 118 different elements that exist in nature. Oxygen (O), nitrogen (N), iron (Fe) and mercury (Hg) are a few examples of elements.

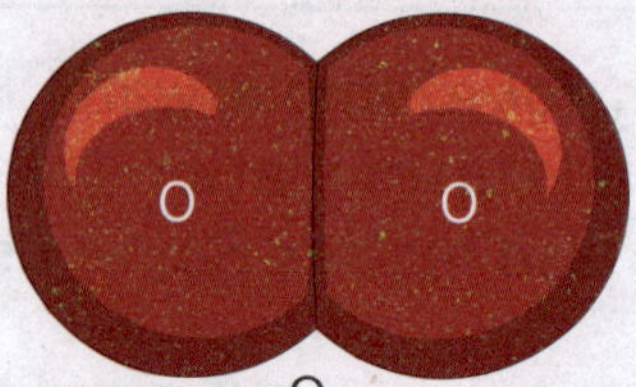

O_2
Oxygen molecule

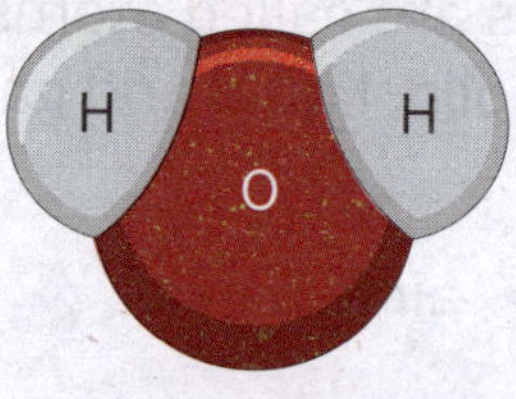

H_2O
Water molecule

▲ Fig. 1.1 Molecules

Elements individually cannot represent all the matter in the universe. They exist in many combinations. Matter in the universe is made up of different elements in various proportions.

When two or more atoms combine, they form a molecule. A **molecule** is the smallest repeating unit of a given substance. A molecule has all the properties of the substance that it forms. The atoms in a molecule are held together by strong chemical bonds. The bond is actually formed by the exchange or sharing of electrons between the atoms.

A molecule can be made up of atoms of the same or different elements. For example,

- An oxygen molecule is made up of two oxygen atoms (O_2). That is, it contains atoms of only the element oxygen.
- A water molecule is made up of two hydrogen atoms and one oxygen atom (H_2O). That is, it contains atoms of both hydrogen and oxygen elements.

Remember

All compounds are molecules. But all molecules are not compounds.

Molecules that contain atoms of at least two different elements are called **compounds**. Water molecule (H_2O) is a compound, but hydrogen molecule (H_2) and oxygen molecule (O_2) are not compounds.

Kinetic Theory of Matter

Kinetic theory of matter states that matter is made up of particles (molecules) and they are always in motion. Kinetic theory explains the properties of the various states of matter.

According to the kinetic theory of matter:

- Molecules in a matter are always in a state of motion.
- The velocity and the kinetic energy of the molecules increase with increase in temperature and vice versa.

- The molecules of matter always attract each other. This force of attraction is called **intermolecular force of attraction**. The force of attraction is maximum between molecules in solid, less in liquids and least in the case of gas molecules.
- There exists space between the molecules of matter. This space between consecutive molecules is called **intermolecular space**. The more the intermolecular space, the less will be the intermolecular force of attraction, and vice versa.

Remember

Kinetic energy of a particle $= \frac{1}{2}mv^2$ where m is the mass and v is the velocity of the particle.

Know the Scientist

Robert Brown (1773–1858) was a Scottish botanist. In 1827, he observed that pollen grains suspended in water showed random, zigzag motion when seen under a microscope. This motion was named as Brownian motion and was later explained through kinetic theory of matter. It confirmed the existence of atoms and molecules and that they are in constant motion.

Revision Zone

Write T for True and F for False.

1. Solids are easily compressible in comparison to gases.
2. Molecules in matter are always in a state of motion.
3. As temperature increases, kinetic energy decreases.
4. A molecule of a compound is made up of atoms of different elements.

Arrangement of Molecules in Matter

Let us look at the arrangement of molecules in the three states of matter.

Solids

In solids, the molecules are closely packed and each molecule has a fixed position. According to kinetic theory, the force of attraction between the molecules of solid is so strong that they cannot move freely, but they constantly vibrate. That is, each molecule vibrates about its fixed position with small amplitudes. Consequently, solids are rigid and have a definite shape and volume. Solids can change their shape only when a very large force is applied to them, like hammering or squeezing. When solids are heated, the amplitude of vibration of molecules increases and when solids are cooled the amplitude of vibration decreases.

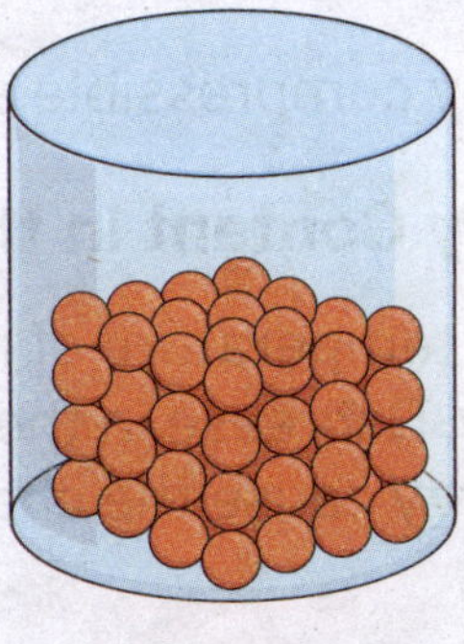

▲ Fig. 1.2 Arrangement of molecules in solids

Characteristics of Solids

- Have a fixed shape, size and volume
- Intermolecular forces are strong

- The molecules vibrate about their fixed positions
- Not easily compressible and do not flow

Liquids

In liquids, the molecules are closely packed (but slightly further apart compared to solids), with little empty space between them. The force of attraction between the liquid molecules is strong but not as strong as in solids. So, the molecules can move around in the substance, but cannot leave the substance. They can slide past each other and hence, liquids maintain their volume but not their shape (they take the shape of the container in which they are filled). Liquids are more compressible and less dense than solids.

▲ Fig. 1.3 Arrangement of molecules in liquids

Characteristics of Liquids

- Have fixed volume but no fixed shape
- Intermolecular forces are strong but not as strong as in solids
- The molecules slide past each other
- Not easily compressible but flow easily

Gases

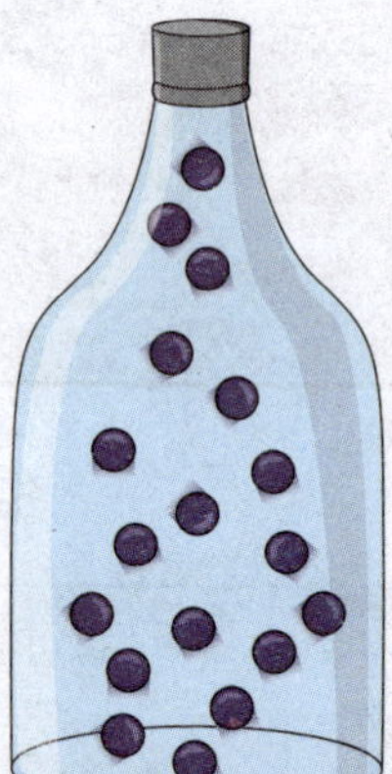

▲ Fig. 1.4 Arrangement of molecules in gases

In gases, the molecules are loosely packed because gases have negligible intermolecular forces of attraction and this enables gas molecules to move around freely. Thus, the intermolecular distance between gas molecules is higher than in solids and liquids. Consequently, gas molecules are always flowing, highly compressible and do not have a fixed volume or shape. Gas molecules move randomly and always collide with each other and with the walls of the container that they are filled in. Whatever the shape and volume of the container, the gas molecules spread out completely to fill it.

Characteristics of Gases

- Do not have fixed volume and shape
- Intermolecular forces are weaker than in solids and liquids
- The molecules move around easily
- Easily compressible and flow freely

Energy Content in the Three States of Matter

As the temperature of matter increases, particles move quickly because they have more energy. Decrease in the temperature results in slower movement of particles. These changes in energy cause the changes in the states of matter.

In a solid, particles have less energy. They are tightly packed together (more dense), and cannot move freely. That is why, solids have a definite shape and volume.

In a liquid, particles have more energy. They are less tightly packed (less dense), and can move freely. Liquids have definite volume but no definite shape. They take the shape of the container.

In a gas, particles have maximum energy. They move freely and spread out rapidly. Gases do not have a definite shape or volume and can expand to fill the entire container. Thus, as the temperature of matter increases, its density decreases (particles move apart).

Let us take the example of ice. The substance ice in the solid state. In solid state the particles/molecules are very tightly packed in a regular pattern. The molecules cannot move freely. They can move around very little. They have a low amount of energy.

When ice is heated, the molecules get more energy and start moving around faster and smoothly against each other. The state changes from solid to liquid and ice changes to water. Hence, molecules in a liquid have more energy than molecules in a solid.

On providing more heat to the water, the molecules start moving faster and they cannot be held together at all. The molecules in the gas have the most energy.

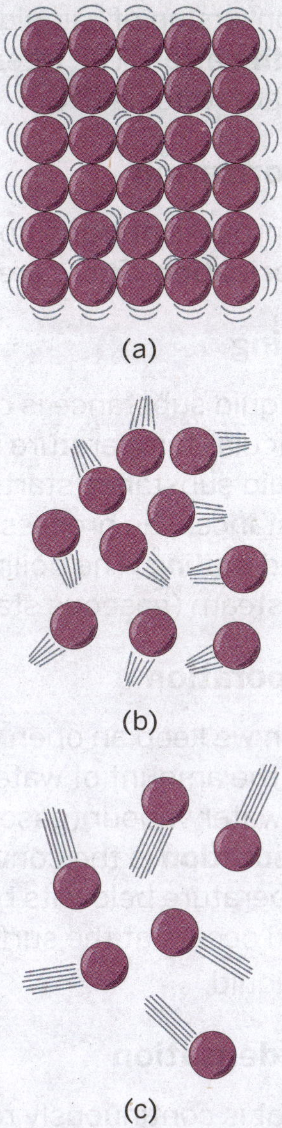

▲ Fig. 1.5 Movement of particles in (a) solids (b) liquids and (c) gases

Change of State

We know that matter exists in three states: solid, liquid and gas. We can change the state of certain substances by supplying heat energy to the substance or by removing heat energy from the substance. The change of state of a substance is also called **change of phase**.

Melting

If a solid substance is continuously supplied heat energy, its temperature increases and at a particular temperature it gets converted to its liquid state. The process of conversion of a solid into its liquid state is called **fusion** or **melting**. The constant temperature at which a solid substance starts converting to its liquid state is called the **melting point** of that substance. The melting point of ice is 0°C. That is, ice (solid state) gets converted into water (liquid state) at its melting point 0°C.

Freezing

If heat is continuously removed from a liquid, its temperature decreases and it converts into its solid state at a constant temperature that is called its **freezing point**. This process of conversion of a liquid into its solid state at its freezing point is called **freezing** or **solidification**. The freezing point of a substance is the same as its melting point. The freezing point of water is 0°C.

Vaporization

The process of transition of a substance from its liquid state to its gaseous state is called **vaporization**. There are two ways in which vaporization takes place: boiling and evaporation.

Boiling

If a liquid substance is continuously supplied heat energy, its temperature increases and at a particular temperature it starts converting into its gaseous state. The temperature at which a liquid substance starts converting into its gaseous state is called the **boiling point** of the substance. The process of conversion of a liquid into its gaseous state at its boiling point is called **boiling**. The boiling point of water is 100°C. That is, water (liquid state) gets converted into steam (gaseous state) at its boiling point 100°C.

Evaporation

When we keep an open container filled with water in a room for some time, we observe that the amount of water in the container decreases after some time. The water converts into water vapour (gaseous state) even before it boils. This process is called evaporation. **Evaporation** is the conversion of a substance from its liquid state into gaseous state at a temperature below its boiling point. Evaporation is different from boiling as evaporation of a liquid occurs at the surface of the liquid, whereas boiling occurs through the entire volume of the liquid.

Condensation

If heat is continuously removed from a gaseous substance, its temperature decreases and it gets converted into its liquid state at a particular temperature called the **condensation point**, which is the same as its boiling point. The process of conversion of a gas into its liquid state at its condensation point is called **condensation**. The condensation point of steam is 100°C. That is, when steam (gaseous state) is cooled, it starts converting into water (liquid state) at 100°C.

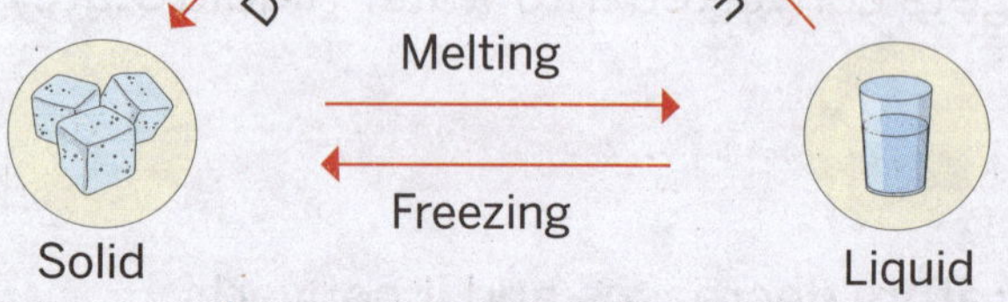

▲ Fig. 1.6 Change of state

Sublimation

Some solid substances like camphor, naphthalene and iodine get converted into their gaseous state without undergoing the liquid state. This process is called **sublimation**. When a gas gets converted into a solid without undergoing its liquid state, it is called **deposition** or **desublimation**. It is the reverse of sublimation. An example of deposition is the conversion of water vapour in air to ice without first becoming a liquid during winter season.

Fig. 1.6 shows the various changes of states.

Activity 1

Aim: To show the melting of solids on heating and freezing of liquids on cooling

Materials required: Stove, paraffin wax, glass and pan

Procedure:

Place some pieces of paraffin wax in the glass. Keep the glass in the pan. Place the pan on the stove and heat. Observe the changes in the paraffin wax. Now, turn off the stove and allow the wax to cool down. Observe the changes in the paraffin wax.

Observation:

Process	Changes observed
Heating	
Cooling	

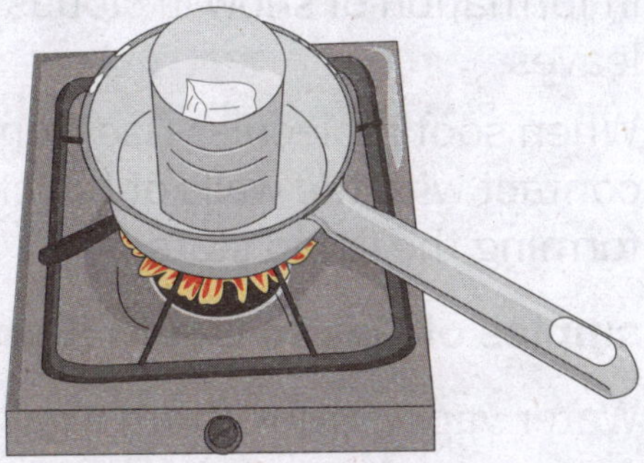

Conclusion:

- Solids get converted into liquids upon heating.
- Liquids get converted into solids upon cooling.

Science in Context

The melting point and the boiling point of a substance depend on atmospheric pressure. When we go to higher altitudes, the atmospheric pressure decreases. Consequently, the melting and the boiling points of a substance also decrease. Hence, their values are lower at higher altitudes than at sea level.

Interconversion of the Three States of Matter

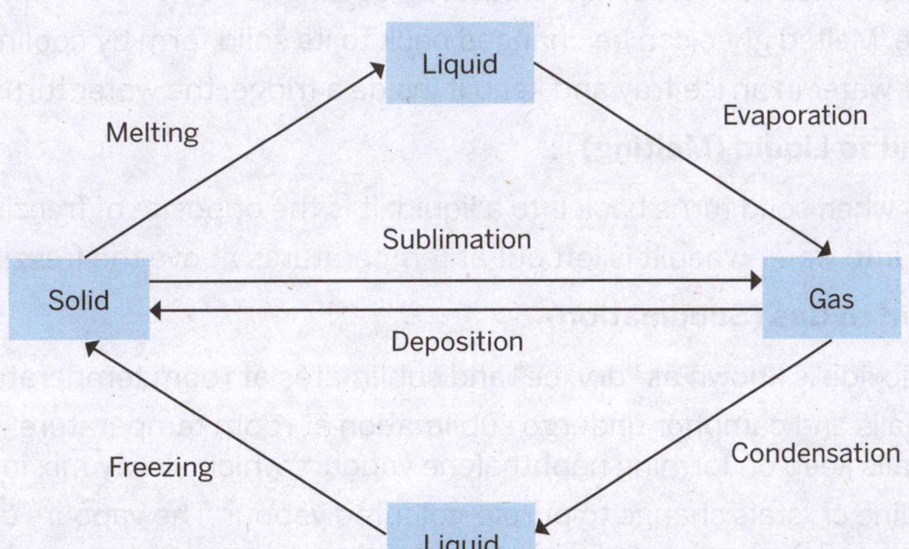

Interconversion of three states of matter

In most cases, solids turn into gases only after an intermediate liquid state.

There are many examples of matter going through each of these transitions.

Examples of Gas to Solid (Deposition)

Under certain circumstances, gas can transform directly into a solid. This process is called deposition.

- In sub-freezing air, water vapour changes directly to ice without becoming a liquid, resulting in formation of snow in clouds. This is also how frost forms on the ground or on surface of leaves.
- When soot molecules rise from the fire, they are in a hot and gaseous state. On coming in contact with the walls of the chimney, they cool down and change to the solid state, without forming the liquid state.

Examples of Gas to Liquid (Condensation)

- Water vapour turns from a gas into a liquid, such as formation of dew on the morning grass.
- Water vapour forms water droplets on the outer surface of a glass of a cold beverage.
- The water vapour in air condenses and we get the same water in the form of rain.

Examples of Liquid to Gas (Vaporization)

- Water is vaporized when it is boiled on a stove to cook vegetables or rice.
- Water evaporates from a pond or a pool during hot summer months.
- Separation of salt from sea water.
- When wet clothes are spread out on a clothesline, the water gets evaporated, making the clothes dry.

Examples of Liquid to Solid (Freezing)

- We can get the solid ice back from liquid water by cooling it.
- Melting of ghee. Melted ghee can be changed back to its solid form by cooling.
- When you pour water in an ice tray and keep it inside a fridge, the water turns into ice cubes.

Examples of Solid to Liquid (Melting)

- Melting occurs when solid turns back into a liquid; it is the opposite of freezing.
- Ice melts back into water when it is left out at temperatures above the freezing point.

Examples of Solid to Gas (Sublimation)

- Solid carbon dioxide is known as "dry ice" and sublimates at room temperature.
- Naphthalene balls and camphor undergo sublimation at room temperature. The naphthalene balls keep on forming naphthalene vapours which slowly mix in the air.
- On heating, iodine crystals change to purple-coloured vapour. The vapours change back to solid form (crystals) when cooled. This process is called sublimation in which a solid directly changes into its gaseous form.

Activity 2

Aim: To show that temperature remains constant during melting and boiling

Materials required: Beaker 500 ml, Bunsen burner, tripod stand, thermometer, ice cubes and water.

Procedure:

1. Place the ice cubes in the beaker and keep it on the tripod stand. Use the thermometer to note the initial temperature of the ice in the beaker.
2. Heat the ice in the beaker using the Bunsen burner. Note the temperature when the ice starts melting.
3. Continue heating till the water starts boiling and note the temperature.

Observation: The temperature first increases and then remains constant when the ice starts melting. The temperature again increases and remains constant when the water starts boiling.

Conclusion: Temperature remains constant during change of state of a substance.

Activity 3

Aim: To show that water will evaporate from our finger

Materials required: A cup of water

Procedure:

1. Dip your index finger in water, then hold it up and keep it like that till it becomes dry.
2. What do you see and feel?

Observation: The water evaporates from your finger, leaving it dry. Your finger also feels cold. This is because the heat from your body is transferred to the liquid water and carried away in water vapour.

Note: This experiment is best done outdoors or somewhere where there is a draft, such as an open window.

Revision Zone

Fill in the blanks

1. The process in which solids are converted into liquids is called ________________ (melting/freezing).
2. The process in which liquids are converted into gases is called ________________ (vaporization/condensation).
3. When a gas gets converted into a solid without undergoing its liquid state, it is called ________________ (deposition/sublimation).

Keywords

Atoms: the basic building blocks of matter

Intermolecular forces: force of attraction between atoms or molecules

Element: a substance that has all the atoms of the same type

Molecule: the smallest repeating unit of a given substance, formed when two or more atoms combine

Compound: a molecule that contains atoms of at least two different elements

Fusion/Melting: process of conversion of a solid into a liquid

Freezing: process of conversion of a liquid into a solid

Condensation: process of conversion of a gas into a liquid

Evaporation: slow conversion of a liquid into a gas below its boiling point

Sublimation: conversion of a solid into a gas without undergoing the liquid state

Deposition: conversion of a gas into its solid state without undergoing its liquid state

In a Nutshell

- Kinetic theory of matter states that all molecules in matter are in a state of continuous motion.
- In a solid, particles have less energy. They are tightly packed together (more dense), and cannot move freely. Solids have a definite shape and volume.
- In a liquid, particles have more energy. They are less tightly packed (less dense), and can move freely. Liquids have definite volume but no definite shape. They take the shape of the container.
- In a gas, particles have maximum energy. They move freely and spread out rapidly. Gases do not have a definite shape or volume and can expand to fill the entire container. Thus, as the temperature of matter increases, its density decreases (particles move apart).
- The state of matter changes when it is heated or cooled.

Exercise

1 Choose the correct answer for each of the following.

a. In which of the following states are the molecules always in a state of motion?

i. Solids ii. Liquids
iii. Gases iv. All of these

b. Identify the type of matter in which intermolecular forces are the weakest.

i. Solids ii. Liquids
iii. Gases iv. All of these

c. Identify the process by which liquids are converted into gases.

i. Melting ii. Freezing
iii. Condensation iv. Vaporization

d. In which of the following is conduction the primary mode of heat transfer?

i. Solids ii. Liquids
iii. Gases iv. All of these

e. The process of conversion of a liquid into a solid is called

i. sublimation ii. condensation
iii. freezing iv. fusion

f. The process of conversion of a solid into a gas without undergoing its liquid state is called

i. evaporation ii. fusion
iii. sublimation iv. condensation

2 Fill in the blanks.

a. Water is an example of ____________ (a molecule/an element).

b. Molecules in matter are always in a state of ____________ (rest/motion).

c. ____________ (Solids/Liquids) have fixed shape and volume.

d. The process of conversion of a gas into a liquid is called ____________ (vaporization/condensation).

e. The conversion of a substance from its liquid state into its gaseous state at a temperature below its boiling point is called ____________ (boiling/evaporation).

3 Write T for True and F for False.

a. An element is a substance that has only similar type of atoms.

b. Solids are highly compressible compared to liquids and gases.

c. The conversion of a substance from its liquid state to its solid state is called solidification.

d. Conversion of liquid into gaseous state is known as freezing.

e. Dew on the morning grass is due to condensation.

4 Define the following.

a. Sublimation

b. Evaporation

c. Freezing

d. Melting

e. Solid

f. Deposition

5 Differentiate between the following.

a. Melting and freezing

b. Boiling and evaporation

c. Vaporization and condensation

d. Sublimation and Deposition

6 Answer the following questions in brief.

a. List any three differences between solids, liquids and gases.

b. Discuss the different change of states of matter briefly.
c. Suggest an activity to show how solids change to liquid and liquids change to gases.
d. Give reason: why does a naphthalene ball disappear if left in open for some days?
e. Give reason: why are we able to sense the smell of a perfume sprayed at a distance?

❼ Answer the following questions in detail.

a. State the postulates of kinetic theory.
b. Explain the characteristics of solids, liquids and gases.
c. What is vaporization? Give two examples.
d. List few examples of deposition, condensation, sublimation.
e. Illustrate the interconversion of states of matter with the help of a diagram.

❽ Think and answer.

If the incense stick is lighted and kept in one room, we can smell it from the other room. Why?

❾ Project

Take two beakers, one filled with water at 25 °C (room temperature) and other with water at 60 °C. Pour a drop of ink in both the beakers and find out in which of the two, ink disperses at a faster rate turning the water completely blue.

Worksheet

A Subject Integration

Depict the movement of the particles for the given change of states of matter.

1. Boiling

2. Evaporation

3. Freezing

B Life Skills

To inflate and deflate a balloon using different states of matter

Materials Required: Soda/Soft drink bottle, balloon, trough of water, Bunsen burner and stand.

Procedure: Fix a balloon on the mouth of a bottle (un-blown balloon). Place the set up in a trough of water. Observe if any changes happen? Now empty the trough and fill with hot water. Observe the changes. Again in another trough of ice, place the setup and observe the changes.

Physical Quantities and Measurement

2

What I shall learn

- Density
- Relative density
- Floating and sinking
- Comparison of densities in the three states of matter

Introduction

Measurement is the act of determining the magnitude of a physical quantity.

You have learned in the previous classes the act of determining physical quantities such as length, area, mass and volume of solids and liquids, weight of a substance, time and temperature.

Density is a physical quantity which can be determined with the help of mass and weight.

In this chapter, we will learn how to determine density of irregular solids and relative density.

Density

We have learned in the previous classes that the density of a substance is defined as mass per unit volume of the substance. That is,

$$\text{Density} = \frac{\text{mass}}{\text{volume}}$$

The SI unit of mass is kg and that of volume is m^3. Hence, the SI unit of density is **kg/m^3** or $kg\ m^{-3}$.

Measuring Density of Irregular Solids

Density of irregular solids can be measured with the help of an apparatus called Eureka Can, and a measuring cylinder. When an object is dropped in the Eureka Can filled with water, the water displaces through the spout in the Can. This displaced water can be measured using the measuring cylinder which helps in finding the volume of the liquid.

Prerequisite Knowledge

Density of a substance is its mass per unit volume, i.e.,

$$\text{Density} = \frac{\text{mass}}{\text{volume}}$$

where, mass can be measured using weighing scale and volume can be known by using measuring cylinders.

The following activity shows how density of an irregular solid can be calculated.

Activity 1

Aim: To measure the density of an irregular solid

Material required: Irregular solid (Stone), weighing scale, Eureka Can and measuring cylinder.

Method:

1. Measure and note down the mass of the irregular solid (in grams).
2. Pour water into the Eureka Can until some spills out into the measuring cylinder.
3. When the water stops spilling out, you will see that the level of water is exactly the same as the level of spout.
4. Examine the level of water in the measuring cylinder and write down the value.
5. Tie the irregular solid with a thread and slowly put it to the bottom of the Eureka Can, carefully. The water will splash into the measuring cylinder.
6. Note down the new value of the water collected in the measuring cylinder.
7. Subtract the two values, the answer is the volume of the irregular solid which can be substituted in the formula below, to find out the density.

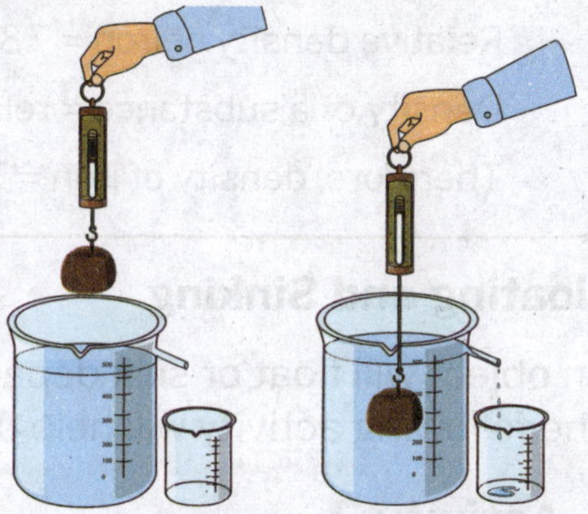

Result: Density is calculated by using the formula,

$$\text{Density} = \frac{\text{mass}}{\text{volume}} \text{ g cm}^{-3}$$

Repeat the procedure using irregular solids made of different materials and make a note of different values of density.

Conclusion: The density of an irregular solid can be found by substituting the values of mass and volume in the formula of the density.

Relative Density

The density of a material with respect to the density of water is known as its **relative density**. It is the ratio of the density of a substance to the density of water.

$$\text{Relative density of a substance} = \frac{\text{density of the substance}}{\text{density of water}}$$

It is also known as **specific gravity**. Since relative density is a pure ratio, it has no unit. The density of water is 1000 kg/m^3 or 1 g/cm^3. So, it is easier to compare the density of a substance with that of water. If the relative density of a substance is known, the density of the substance can be found out using the formula,

Density of a substance = relative density of the substance × density of water

Solved Problems

1. Find the relative density of kerosene. The density of kerosene is 810 kg/m^3 and the density of water is 1000 kg/m^3.

   Solution:

   Density of kerosene = 810 kg/m^3, density of water = 1000 kg/m^3

   $$\text{Relative density of a substance} = \frac{\text{density of the substance}}{\text{density of water}}$$

   $$\text{Therefore, relative density of kerosene} = \frac{810}{1000} = 0.81$$

2. The relative density of iron is 7.87. Find the density of iron.

   Solution:

   Relative density of iron = 7.87, density of water = 1000 kg/m^3

   Density of a substance = relative density of the substance × density of water

   Therefore, density of iron = 7.87×1000 kg/m^3 = 7870 kg/m^3

Floating and Sinking

An object will float or sink depending on its density and the density of the liquid it is placed in. The following activity will help us understand floating and sinking.

Activity 2

Aim: To understand floating and sinking with respect to density

Materials required: Two beakers, water, kerosene, wooden block and iron nail

Procedure:

Case 1:

Fill two beakers with water. Place the wooden block in one beaker and the iron nail in the other beaker. Observe what happens in both the beakers.

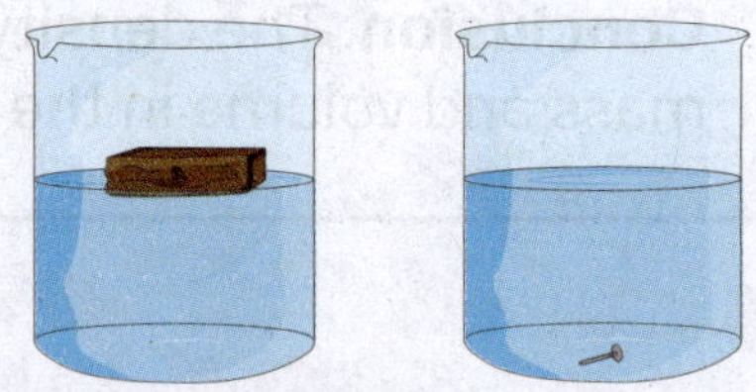

Fig. a

Observation and conclusion:

The wooden block floats on water as its density is less than water. The iron nail sinks as its density is more than water (Fig. a).

Case 2:

Fill one beaker with water and one with kerosene. Place the wooden block first in water and then in kerosene. Observe what happens to the block when placed in both the beakers.

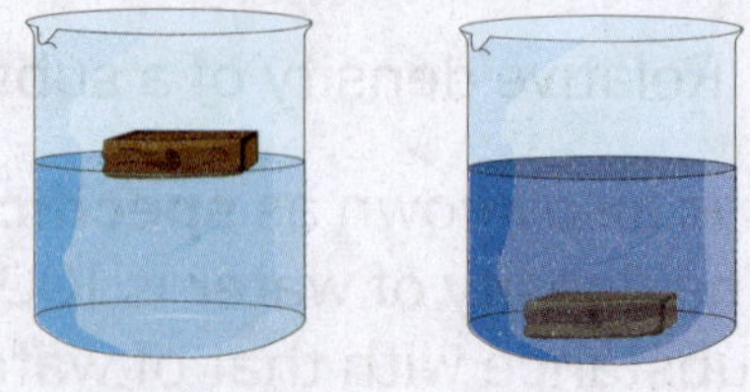

Fig. b

Observation and conclusion:

The wooden block floats on water as its density is less than water. It sinks in kerosene as its density is more than kerosene (Fig. b).

Do You Know?

Balloons used for advertisements are filled with helium and fly higher than normal balloons filled with air. This is because helium is less dense than air. So, it floats over air.

From Activity 2, we can conclude that:

- An object will float on a liquid if its density is less than liquid.
- An object will sink in a liquid if its density is more than liquid.

Therefore, to determine if the density of an object is more or less than a liquid, check if it floats or sinks in the liquid.

A liquid substance can also float or sink in another liquid depending on the densities of the liquids. Let us understand this with the help of an activity.

Activity 3

Aim: To compare the densities of cooking oil and water

Materials required: Two glass bottles, water and cooking oil

Procedure:

1. Fill half a bottle with water.
2. Then, pour some cooking oil into it.
3. Now, fill the second bottle with cooking oil and then add water.
4. Observe the behaviour of the cooking oil.

Observation: The cooking oil always floats on the surface of water.

Conclusion: Density of water is more than the density of cooking oil.

Science in Context

The **Dead Sea**, also known as the Salt Sea, is actually a salt lake bordered by Jordan, Israel and Palestine. High concentration of salt content in the Dead Sea water makes its density almost 24% higher than regular water. Because of this reason, anyone can float in the Dead Sea water.

Relative Density Bottle

Relative density of a liquid can be determined using a relative density bottle. Relative density bottle is also known as **specific gravity bottle**. It is a glass bottle of fixed capacity. It has a glass stopper with a fine hole (capillary tube). When the bottle is filled with a liquid and closed with the stopper, the excess liquid rises through the fine hole and runs down outside. This ensures that the bottle holds only a fixed volume of a liquid.

The following activity will help us to understand the steps to find the relative density of a liquid using a relative density bottle.

▲ Fig. 2.1 Relative density bottle

Activity 4

Aim: To determine the relative density of a liquid using the relative density bottle

Materials required: Relative density bottle, physical balance, water and liquid of which relative density has to be determined

Procedure:

1. Weigh the empty relative density bottle using a physical balance and note down the mass as M_1.
2. Fill the bottle with water and close it with a stopper. The excess water will drain out of the bottle.
3. Note down the mass of the relative density bottle with water as M_2 and empty the bottle.
4. Fill it with a liquid whose relative density is to be measured.
5. Close the bottle with the glass stopper. Once the excess liquid drains out, note down the mass of the relative density bottle with the liquid as M_3.

Observation and conclusion:

Mass of the liquid, $m_\ell = M_3 - M_1 =$ ____________

Mass of water, $m_w = M_2 - M_1 =$ ____________

Relative density of a liquid is given as the ratio of the masses of the liquid and water at a constant volume.

Let us prove this. Let V be the volume of the relative density bottle.

$$\text{Density of the liquid} = \frac{\text{mass}}{\text{volume}} = \frac{m_\ell}{V}$$

$$\text{Density of water} = \frac{m_w}{V}$$

$$\text{Relative density of the liquid} = \frac{\text{density of the liquid}}{\text{density of water}} = \frac{m_\ell/V}{m_w/V}$$

$$= \frac{m_\ell}{m_w} = \text{\_\_\_\_\_\_\_\_\_\_\_\_}$$

Comparison of Densities in the Three States of Matter

We have learned about the arrangement of particles in different states of matter such as solids, liquids and gases. These particles are always in motion. In solids, the particles vibrate about their fixed positions and in liquids and gases, the particles are in random motion.

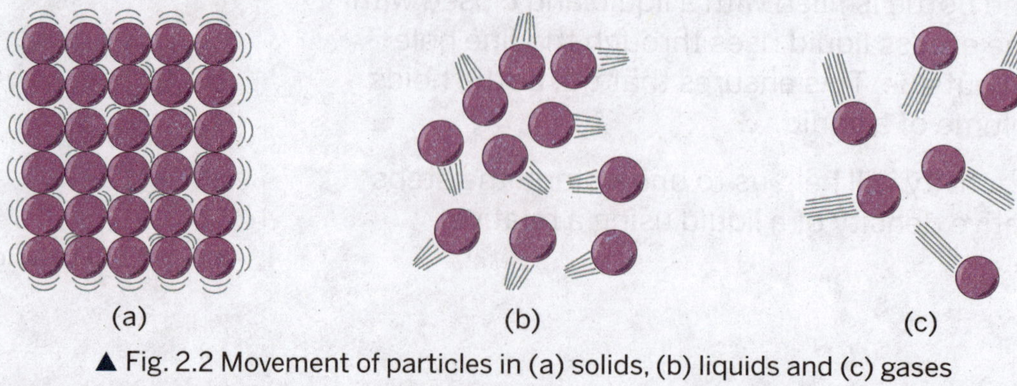

(a) (b) (c)

▲ Fig. 2.2 Movement of particles in (a) solids, (b) liquids and (c) gases

When a substance is heated or cooled, the motion of the particles changes. When heated, particles vibrate faster and move away from each other. When cooled, the vibrating particles slow down and come closer to each other. Hence, the volume of a substance increases when it is heated and decreases when it is cooled. In other words, a substance expands upon heating and contracts upon cooling.

Heating and cooling of substances, thus, change the density of substances. When heated, the density decreases since the particles move away from each other. When cooled, the density increases since the particles come close to each other.

Convection

Convection is a mode of heat transfer through the movement of particles in a substance. Since the particles in liquids and gases are loosely packed and can move around, convection is the primary mode of heat transfer in them.

How Convection Takes Place?

- When a fluid (liquid or gas) is heated, the molecules near the bottom (source of heat) will receive more heat and become lighter.
- These hot and lighter fluid molecules at the bottom then rise up. (Note: A less dense substance always floats over a denser substance.)
- As the hot and lighter fluid rises up, the cooler and denser fluid from the top moves downwards to the bottom, which is vacated by the hot fluid.
- The fluid that comes down is then heated up and rises up which is then replaced by a comparatively cooler fluid at the top.
- This ongoing process sets up circulating streams of hot and cold fluid. This continuous circulatory motion of the fluid is known as **convection current**.

Applications of Convection

Convection is the reason behind boiling of water. The water at the bottom of the kettle gets heated and rises up, while the cooler water at the top of the kettle moves down, which in turn gets heated and moves up. By then, the initially heated water at the top of the kettle cools down. This cold water then moves down. This way the entire volume of water in the kettle heats up. We can see a continuous circular movement of water from top to bottom (convection current) when it boils.

Science in Context

Some objects sink in water because their density is more than that of water. We have noted that solids are denser than water. Then why does ice float on water? We know that density of ice is less than water even though it is the solid state of water. The reason for this is that water has an abnormal behavior (anomalous expansion) between the temperatures 0 °C and 4 °C. So, when water is cooled below 4 °C, it expands rather than contracting. Therefore, the density of water decreases when it freezes to form ice at 0 °C. Thus the density of ice is less than that of water and it floats on water.

Remember

A substance expands upon heating and contracts upon cooling.

▲ Fig. 2.3 Convection current during the boiling of water

The formation of land breeze and sea breeze in coastal regions are examples of convection in air.

Some of the practical applications of convection are:

- Room heaters are placed on the floor of a room which, makes hot air to rise up and effectively heat the entire room.
- The ventilators of a room are at the top of a window or the door for the hot air in the room to rise up and move out.

Revision Zone

Write T for True for F for False.

1. Density of irregular solids can be measured with the help of an apparatus called Eureka Can.
2. Relative density of a substance is the ratio of the density of water to the density of the substance.
3. Cooking oil floats on water since its density is less than water.
4. When a substance is heated, the vibration of the particles in it become faster.
5. Convection is the primary mode of heat transfer in solids.

Keywords

Density: mass per unit volume

Relative density: ratio of the density of a substance to the density of water

Relative density bottle: apparatus used to find relative density

Convection current: the continuous circulatory motion of a fluid when it is heated

In a Nutshell

- Heating and cooling of substances change the density of the substances.
- A substance expands upon heating and contracts upon cooling.
- Convection is the mode of transfer of heat by the movement of particles in liquids and gases.
- Relative density is also known as specific gravity.
- An object will float or sink depending on its density and the density of the liquid it is placed in.

Exercise

1 Choose the correct answer for each of the following.

a. To determine the density of a solid, we have to determine its

i. mass and area

ii. mass and volume

iii. weight and area

iv. weight and volume

b. Which among the following has no unit?

i. Mass

ii. Volume

iii. Relative density

iv. Density

c. The formula used to calculate the density of a substance is

i. $D = mV$ ii. $D = \frac{m}{V}$

iii. $D = \frac{V}{m}$ iv. $D = mV^2$

d. The SI unit of density is

i. kg/m^3 ii. g/m^3

iii. kg/m^2 iv. g/m^2

e. When a substance is heated, its density

i. increases ii. decreases

iii. remains the same iv. none of these

2 Fill in the blanks.

a. The relative density of a liquid is determined by using ____________ (relative density bottle/ specific heat bottle).

b. A wooden block ____________ (floats on/sinks in) water.

c. Relative density bottle is also known as ____________ (specific heat bottle/ specific gravity bottle).

d. The continuous movement of a fluid when it is heated is called ____________ (convection/ conduction) current.

e. Placing a room heater nearer to the ____________ (floor/ceiling) is better.

3 Write T for True and F for False.

a. The SI unit of relative density is kg/m^3.

b. With the rise in temperature of a liquid its density increases.

c. A body having density less than $1\ g/cm^3$ floats in water.

d. Equal volumes of water and kerosene have equal masses.

e. The particles in solids are always in random motion.

4 Define the following.

a. Relative Density bottle

b. Density

c. Relative density

d. Convection

5 Differentiate between the following.

a. Density and relative density

b. Density of water and cooking oil

c. Effect of temperature on solids and liquids

6 Answer the following questions in one sentence each.

a. Name the device used to measure the volume of an irregular solid.

b. List any two examples of substances that float on water.

c. What is specific gravity?

d. Name the device used to determine the relative density of a liquid.

7 Answer the following questions in brief.

a. How do you find density of a substance, if relative density of the substance and density of water is known?

b. When does a substance sink in a liquid?

c. What is convection current?

d. Mention few applications of convection in our daily life?

8 Answer the following questions in detail.

a. Suggest an activity to understand floating and sinking with respect to density.

b. How will you prove that the density of cooking oil is less than that of water?

c. Explain the procedure to find out the relative density of a liquid.

d. Explain how convection causes the boiling of water.

9 Solve the following numerical problems.

a. Calculate the density of a substance whose mass is 10 kg and volume is 2 m^3.

b. Find the mass of a ball whose volume is 200 cm^3 and density is 3 g/cm^3.

c. Find the volume of a substance whose mass is 5 g and density is 50 g/cm^3.

d. Find the relative density of a liquid substance whose density is 920 kg/m^3.

e. Find the density of a substance whose relative density is 1.43.

f. Calculate the density of a substance whose mass is 5.4 g and volume is 2 cm^3.

10 Think and answer.

a. A piece of iron floats on mercury.

b. It is easier to swim in sea than in river. Why?

11 Project

Take different liquids like water, kerosene, cooking oil, corn syrup and fruit juices, and mix them separately with different food colours. Pour all the coloured liquids one by one in a beaker. Note the colour change in each of the liquids. Some of the liquids will not mix and instead form a colourful layer. Discuss the reason behind the layer formation. After this, measure the relative density of each liquid using a specific gravity bottle.

12 In the Library

Try to learn more about the following topics.

- Buoyancy of a liquid
- Density of gases

Worksheet

Solve the problems given below.

{Hint: Density, D = m/v}

1. The volume of a certain wooden block is 63 cm^3. The mass is 11.392 g. Find the density.

2. Calculate the density of a material that has a mass of 53 g and a volume of 14 cm^3.

3. A student finds a rock on the way to school. In the laboratory, he determines that the volume of the rock is 22.5 cm^3, and the mass in 38.943 g. What is the density of the rock?

4. If 31 g of a liquid occupy a space of 35 mℓ. What is the density of the liquid in g/cm^3?

Force and Pressure

3

What I shall learn

- Turning effect of force
- Pressure
- Liquid pressure
- Archimedes' principle
- Pressure exerted by gases
- Atmospheric pressure

Introduction

We are familiar with force and the different effects of force. Identify the effect brought about by force in each of the cases given below.

____

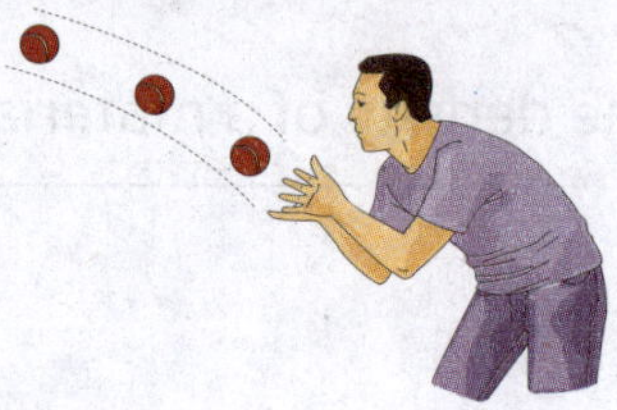

____

____

The effects produced by a force on an object depend on the magnitude of the force applied on the body. For example, if you press a ball between both your hands, the shape of the ball changes. If you press the ball with more force, the ball will be compressed more.

Is there any factor on which the effect of a force depends? Let us find out in this chapter.

Turning Effect of Force

Turning effect of a force is called **moment of force**. When a force causes an object to turn, this turning effect of a force around a fixed point or a fixed axis is called **moment**. A point around which the rotation occurs is called **pivot**. For example, a door opening around a fixed hinge, a spanner turning around a fixed nut, a wrench applied to a bolt or nut, etc.

The moment of force is determined by the product of force and distance arm. The distance arm or moment arm or lever arm is the perpendicular distance between line of action of force and pivot.

Moment = Force X distance arm

or M = F X d

The SI unit of moment is newton-metre (Nm). A moment of 1 Nm is produced by a force of 1 N acting perpendicular to the distance arm 1 m long.

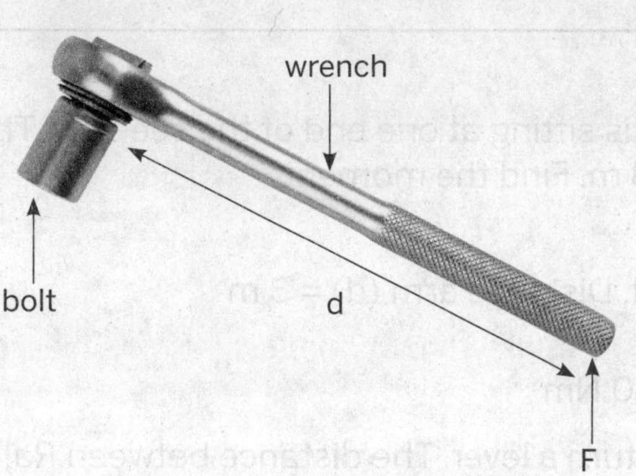

▲ Fig. 3.1 A wrench applied to a bolt

It depends on two factors:

- Magnitude of the force acting on the object or applied by the object.
- The distance of the force from the pivot.

Some of the examples of turning effect of force are listed below:

1. The force applied by a girl sitting on a see-saw produces the turning effect that moves see-saw.
2. When we open or close a door by pushing or pulling, it turns the door about its hinge or axis of rotation. Therefore, door is opened or closed due to the turning effect of the force acting on it.
3. Turning effect of the force applied on a pencil helps turning the pencil in a sharpener.
4. Force applied on a doorknob produces the turning effect that helps to turn the doorknob.

▲ Fig. 3.2 Turning effect of force in case of a door

Have you ever thought why the handle of a door is fixed near the edge of a door? We can open or close a door more easily by applying a force at the edge of a door rather than near the hinge. This is because, larger the distance from the axis of rotation, smaller is the force needed to produce the same turning effect in the body. Thus, the location where the force is applied to turn a body is very important.

Let us study the factors on which moment of force depends.

You might have seen that a mechanic uses a spanner to loosen or tighten a nut or a bolt. A spanner having a long arm helps him to do it with greater ease than the one having short arm.

There are two types of moment of force with respect to the direction of rotation it causes.

1. Clockwise moment
2. Anticlockwise moment

When a force causes an object to turn in a clockwise direction, then it is called **clockwise moment**.

When a force causes an object to turn in an anticlockwise direction, then it is called **anticlockwise moment**.

Solved Problems

1. A boy of weight 20 N is sitting at one end of the see-saw. The distance between the boy and the pivot is 3 m. Find the moment.

Solution:

Given: Force (F) = 20 N, Distance arm (d) = 3 m

Moment (M) = F × d

So, M = 20 N × 3 m = 60 Nm

2. Raj applies 200 N to turn a lever. The distance between Raj and the pivot is 40 cm. Find the moment.

Solution:

Given: Force (F) =200 N

Distance (d) = 40 cm= 0.4 m

Moment (M) = F × d

So, M = 200 × 0.4 = 80 Nm

3. A force of 25 N is applied to the end of the spanner, which is 10 cm away from the centre of the nut. Calculate the moment of force.

Solution:

Given: Force (F) = 25 N, Distance (d) = 10 cm = 0.1 m

M = F × d

So, M = 25 × 0.1 = 2.5 Nm

Pressure

The force acting on a unit surface area of an object is called **pressure**. The pressure on a surface depends on the magnitude of the force acting perpendicular to the surface and the area of the surface.

$$\text{Pressure} = \frac{\text{Force}}{\text{Area}}$$

If F is the force and A is the area, then pressure P is given by $P = \frac{F}{A}$

Unit of pressure in SI system is **pascal (Pa)**. One pascal is equal to one newton per square metre.

$1 \text{ Pa} = 1 \text{ N/m}^2$

Variation of Pressure with Force

Pressure is force per unit area. In other words, as long as the surface area remains unchanged, an increase in the force exerted will lead to an increase in pressure or vice-versa.

Challenge Yourself

Which bicycle is easier to ride with less effort among the following?

a. Bicycle with wider tyres

b. Bicycle with narrow tyres

Variation of Pressure with Area

Pressure exerted by a certain force on a surface depends on the area of the surface. If the force acts on a large area, the pressure exerted is less. If the area of the surface is less, then the pressure exerted by the same force is more. That is, pressure exerted by a definite force on a surface decreases with an increase in the area of the surface.

Activity 1

Aim: To show that pressure increases with decrease in area

Materials required: A tray of approximately 10 cm height, wet mud and two identical bricks

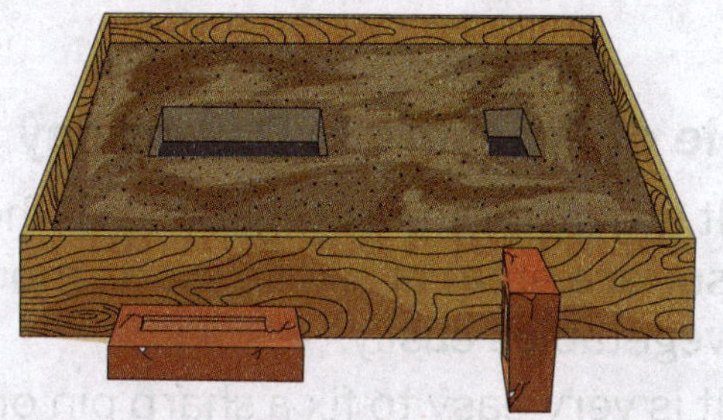

Deeper impression made by the brick with lesser area of contact

Procedure: Fill the tray completely with wet mud (in the paste form) till the brim. Take one brick, label it as 'A' and place it gently on the tray of mud horizontally. Do not press the brick hard. Remove the brick gently from the tray and observe the depth of the impression left behind. Take the second brick, label it as 'B' and place it gently on the same tray of mud, vertically this time. Do not press the brick hard. Remove the brick gently from the tray and observe the depth of the impression left behind.

Record your observations for both the impressions 'A' and 'B'. What do you conclude?

Observations: Brick 'B' makes a deeper impression on the mud compared to brick 'A'.

Conclusion: If the force is constant, pressure increases with decrease in area. As the area of the contact between the brick and wet mud is less for brick 'B' than for brick 'A', brick 'B' makes a deeper impression in the mud.

Solved Problems

1. A man standing in an elevator exerts a force of 600 N on the floor due to his weight. Area of the floor of the elevator is 2 m^2. How much pressure does he exert on the floor?

Solution:

Force exerted by the man on the floor = 600 N

Area of the floor of the elevator = 2 m^2

$$\text{Pressure} = \frac{\text{Force}}{\text{Area}} = \frac{600}{2} = 300 \text{ Pa}$$

2. A girl beats a drum with a force of 300 N. The radius of the circular membrane of the drum is 0.5 m. How much pressure does she exert on the drum?

Solution:

Force exerted by the girl = 300 N

Radius of the membrane of the drum = 0.5 m

Area of the membrane of the drum $= \pi r^2 = 0.785\ m^2$

$$\text{Pressure} = \frac{\text{Force}}{\text{Area}} = \frac{300}{0.785} = 382.17\ \text{Pa}$$

Role of Pressure in Day-to-day Life

- It is difficult to cut vegetables if the knife edge is not sharp. The sharp edge (having less surface area) of a knife exerts more pressure on the vegetables so that the knife pierces the vegetables easily.
- It is very easy to fix a sharp pin on a board since the pressure at the sharp tip is high due to the small area it occupies.
- Straps of school bags are usually broad. This reduces the pressure on the shoulders.
- Camels have broad feet, which help them to walk easily on sand in the desert. Since the area is more, the pressure exerted by their weight on the sand is less. Therefore, their feet do not sink into the sand easily.

Revision Zone

Fill in the blanks with the correct words.

1. The force acting on unit area of a surface is called ________. (pressure/push)
2. The unit of pressure in the SI system is ________ . (N/Pa)
3. Pressure increases with an increase in ________ .(force applied/surface area)
4. It is easy to cut vegetables with a ________ knife. (sharp-edged/blunt)

Liquid Pressure

Liquids exert pressure on the surface of a body immersed in it and on the surface of the container in which they are placed. Let us derive an expression for the pressure exerted by a liquid.

Suppose a liquid of mass m and density ρ is taken in a cylindrical container like a beaker, which has a flat base or bottom (Fig. 3.3). Let A be the area of the base of the container, h be the height of the liquid level in the container from the bottom and V be the volume occupied by the liquid.

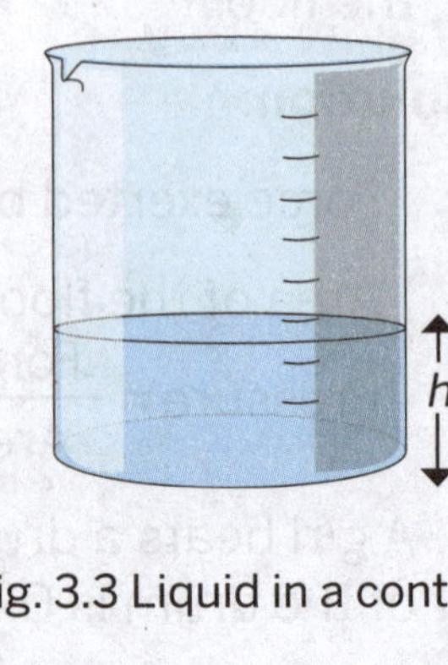

▲ Fig. 3.3 Liquid in a container

The liquid exerts a force that is equal to its weight towards the bottom of the container. The weight of the liquid in the container is

$$W = m \times g$$

Where g is the acceleration due to gravity. Mass = density × volume. So,

$$W = \rho \times V \times g$$

Volume, $V = A \times h$. So,

$$W = \rho \times A \times h \times g$$

Hence, the force exerted by the liquid is

$$F = W = \rho \times A \times h \times g$$

We know that, pressure, $P = \frac{F}{A}$. So, pressure at the bottom of the container due to the liquid is given by

$$P = \frac{\rho \times A \times h \times g}{A} = h\rho g$$

Since acceleration due to gravity is a constant at a given place, the pressure exerted by a liquid depends on the height of the liquid and the density of the liquid.

Properties of Liquid Pressure

- Pressure exerted by a liquid increases with increase in depth from the liquid surface.
- Pressure exerted by a liquid at the same depth will be the same.
- Liquids exert pressure in all directions.

Activity 2

Aim: To show that pressure exerted by liquids increases with increase in depth

Materials required: Transparent plastic bottle or vessel and water

Procedure:

1. Make small holes in the plastic vessel at the positions A, B and C as shown in the figure.
2. Then, fill the vessel with water.
3. Observe the water flowing out through the three holes. What difference do you find in the flow of water through the holes?

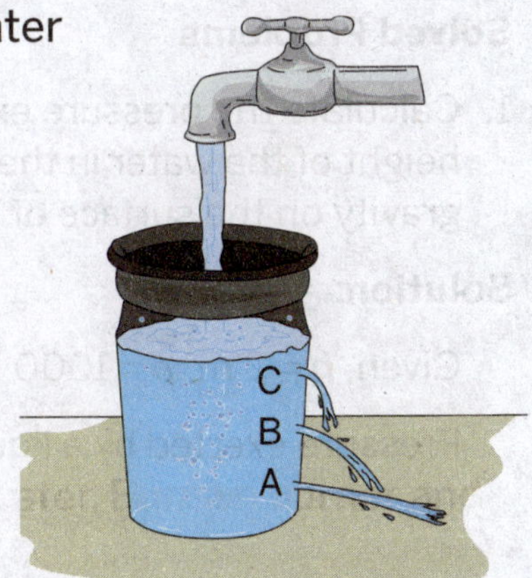

Observation: The horizontal distance at which the water is flowing out is maximum for the hole at A and minimum for the hole at C.

Conclusion: Pressure exerted by liquids increases with depth. Thus pressure at A is maximum due to the largest depth and pressure at C is minimum due to the small depth.

Activity 3

Aim: To show that liquid pressure is the same at equal depth

Materials required: Plastic container, water and needle

Procedure:

1. Make three holes in the plastic container at the same level.
2. Fill the container with water.

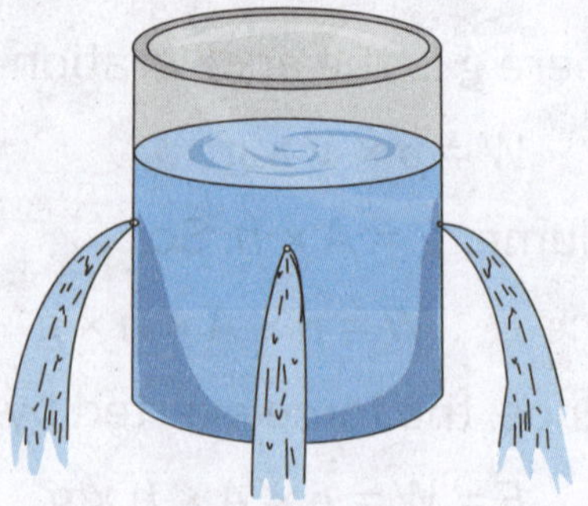

Observation: The water falls at equal horizontal distance from the three holes.

Conclusion: Pressure is the same at equal depth.

Activity 4

Aim: To show that liquids exert pressure in all directions

Materials required: Polythene bag, needle and water

Procedure:

1. Fill the polythene bag with some water.
2. Hold its mouth tightly and then puncture the polythene bag at various places with the needle.

Observation: Water pours out from all the holes.

Conclusion: Liquid exerts pressure in all directions.

Solved Problems

1. Calculate the pressure exerted by the water in a water tank at the bottom of the tank. Given, height of the water in the tank is 2 m, density of water is 1000 kg/m^3 and acceleration due to gravity on the surface of Earth is 9.8 m/s^2.

Solution:

Given, $h = 2$ m, $\rho = 1000$ kg/m^3 and g = 9.8 m/s^2.

Pressure exerted by a liquid, $P = h\rho g$

$= 2 \times 1000 \times 9.8$

$= 19{,}600$ Pa

2. A beaker has mercury up to a height of 4 cm from its bottom. What is the pressure exerted by the mercury column at the bottom of the beaker? Given, acceleration due to gravity on the surface of Earth is 9.8 m/s^2 and density of mercury is 13,600 kg/m^3.

Solution:

Given, h = 4 cm = 0.04 m, $\rho = 13600\ kg/m^3$ and $g = 9.8\ m/s^2$.

Pressure exerted by mercury, $P = h\rho g$

$$= 0.04 \times 13600 \times 9.8$$

$$= 5331.2\ Pa$$

3. The wall at the bottom of a dam can withstand a pressure of 7,84,000 Pa. Calculate the maximum water level above which the dam may collapse. Given, density of water is 1000 kg/m^3 and acceleration due to gravity on the surface of Earth is 9.8 m/s^2.

Solution:

Given, $P = 784000$ Pa, $\rho = 1000\ kg/m^3$ and $g = 9.8\ m/s^2$.

Let h be the height of water corresponding to the maximum pressure (maximum water level).

Pressure exerted by water, $P = h\rho g$. That is,

$$784000 = h \times 1000 \times 9.8$$

So, maximum water level is given by

$$h = \frac{784000}{1000 \times 9.8} = 80\ m$$

Measuring Liquid Pressure

A **manometer** is an instrument used to measure pressure in fluids. A simple manometer is shown in Fig. 3.4. It consists of a U-shaped tube containing a liquid like water. One end of the tube is left open to air and the other end is connected to a rubber tube which is immersed in a trough containing another liquid whose pressure is to be measured.

Initially, the level of water in both the arms of the U-tube is same. When the rubber tube connected to one end of the U-tube is immersed in the given liquid, the liquid pressure forces the liquid level in that arm of the U-tube to go down. Then liquid level in the other arm goes up. If h is the difference in liquid levels in both the arms of the U-tube, the liquid pressure is given by,

$$P = h\rho g$$

where ρ is the density of the liquid and g is the acceleration due to gravity.

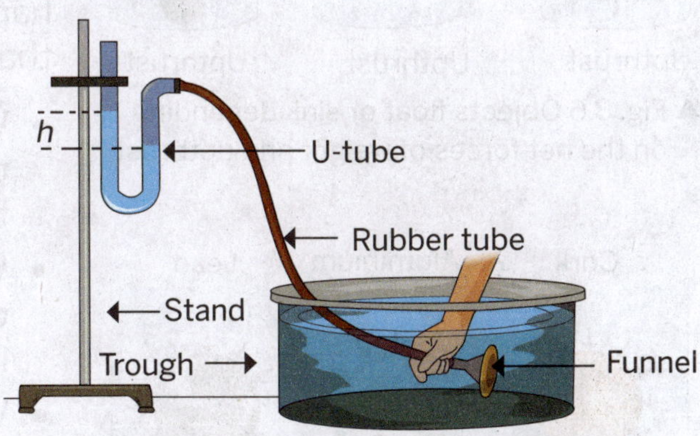

▲ Fig. 3.4 Simple manometer

Archimedes' Principle

When we hold a body immersed in liquid, we feel it is lighter. Why does it happen? If a body is immersed in a liquid, it experiences a resultant upward force against its weight. Therefore, we feel an apparent loss of weight when it is immersed in a liquid. The loss of weight of a body submerged in a liquid is given by Archimedes' principle, which states that the apparent loss of weight of a body fully or partially immersed in a liquid is equal to the weight of the liquid displaced by the body.

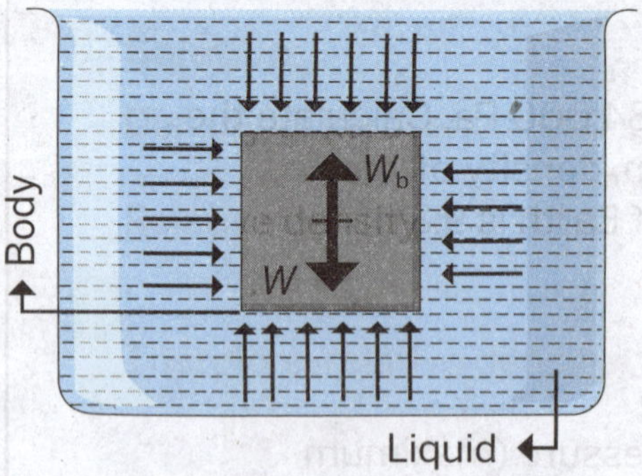

▲ Fig. 3.5 Buoyant force on a body immersed in a liquid

Buoyancy

We know that liquids exert pressure and this pressure increases with depth. If a body is immersed in a liquid, it experiences pressure and hence, force in all directions (Fig. 3.5). The forces acting along both sides get cancelled, whereas the forces acting on the bottom and top of the body do not cancel as they are at different depths inside the liquid. Therefore, the body experiences two forces on it:

- The weight of the body which is acting downwards (W).
- An upward force called **upthrust**. This upthrust on a body immersed in a liquid is called **buoyancy** or **buoyant force** (W_b).

The apparent weight of the body is the difference between the two forces. It is given by

$$W_{apparent} = W - W_b$$

We can note that the apparent weight of the body in a liquid will always be less than its actual weight.

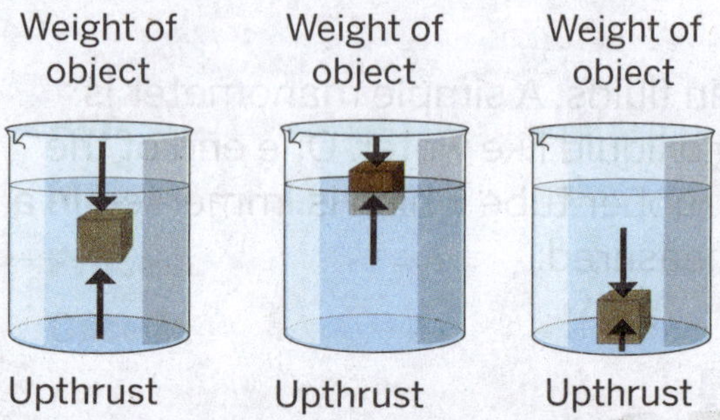

▲ Fig. 3.6 Objects float or sink depending on the net forces of weight and upthrust

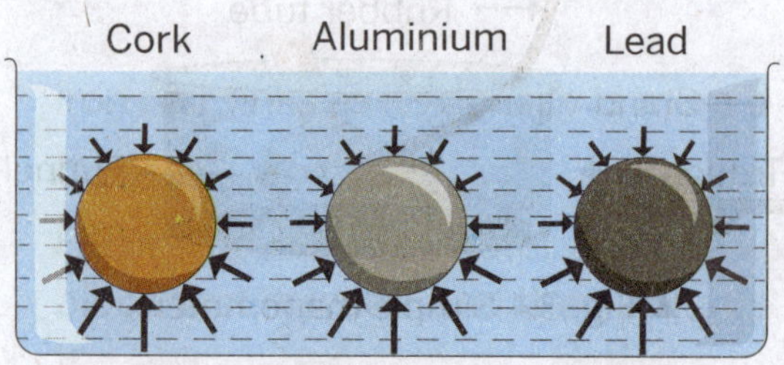

▲ Fig. 3.7 Objects of same volume experience same buoyancy when immersed in the same liquid

Flotation

Some objects sink in water, while some objects float. Why does this happen? An object floats on the surface of a liquid when the weight of the object is less than the weight of the liquid displaced by the object. This happens when the density of the object is less than that of the liquid.

- When the upthrust acting on the object is equal to the weight of the object, the object floats with its top surface just below the free surface of the liquid.
- When the upthrust is more than the weight of the object, then the object floats on the surface of the liquid partially immersed.
- When the upthrust acting on the object is less than the weight of the object, the object sinks in the liquid. In this case, the weight of the liquid displaced by the object is less than the weight of the object (object is denser than the liquid).

The buoyancy experienced by a body does not depend on its weight. Buoyancy depends only on the volume of the body. That is, two bodies having same volume and different weights will experience the same upthrust if immersed in the same liquid. But, whether the object floats or sinks depends on the weight acting against this buoyant force. That is, it is determined by the density of the object.

Activity 5

Aim: To demonstrate the Archimedes' principle

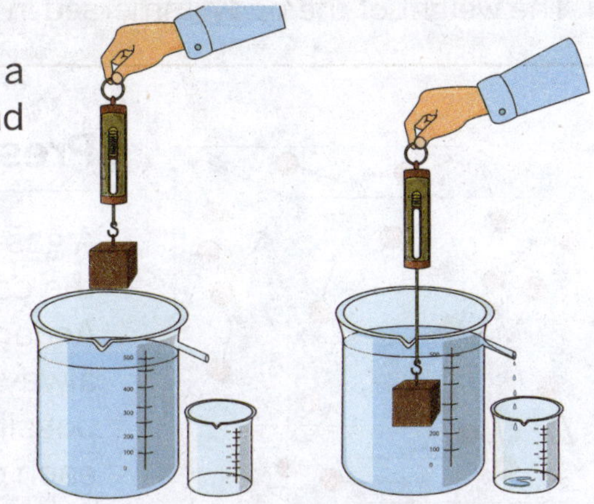

Materials required: Spring balance, big container with a spout at the top, a small beaker, metallic block and thread

Procedure:

1. Hang the metallic block on the spring balance using the thread. Note its weight in air.
2. Fill the big container with water till the spout on its wall.
3. Keep the small beaker near the hole of the big container to collect overflowing water.
4. Immerse the metallic block in water and note the weight of the metallic block in the balance.
5. Collect the water that overflows into the small beaker.
6. Measure the weight of the water collected in the small beaker.
7. Compare the loss of weight of metallic block and the weight of water displaced.

Observation:

Weight of the metallic block in air	
Weight of the metallic block in water	
Weight of the water displaced	

Conclusion: Loss of weight of the object is equal to the weight of the water displaced.

Applications of Archimedes' Principle

- **Submarines**: A submarine adjusts its depth by adjusting the amount of water in its ballast tank. If water is filled in the tank, its weight increases and it sinks. It floats on water by letting the water out, thereby reducing the weight.
- **Ships**: A ship sinks into water only up to a certain level. This is because the weight of the water displaced by the immersed part of the ship is equal to the weight of the ship itself.
- **Hydrometer**: Hydrometer helps us to measure the relative density of liquids. Hydrometer floats in the liquid because the weight of the liquid displaced by its immersed part is equal to its own weight.

Revision Zone

Write T for True and F for False.

1. The gain of weight of a body submerged in a liquid is given by Archimedes' principle.
2. The pressure exerted by a liquid depends on the density of the liquid.
3. The upthrust on a body immersed in a liquid is called buoyancy.
4. The weight of the body immersed in water is equal to the weight of the water displaced.

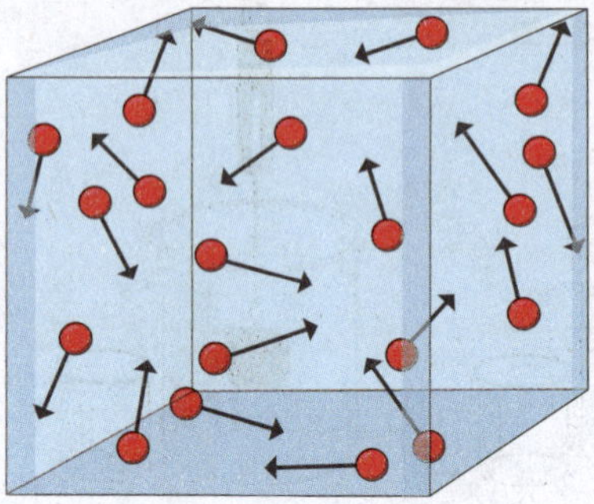

▲ Fig. 3.8 Motion of molecules in a gas

Pressure Exerted by Gases

A gas placed in a container exerts pressure on the walls of the container. A gas contains very large number of molecules. According to kinetic theory of gases, these gas molecules are always in random motion in all possible directions with all possible velocities. While in random motion, they collide with each other and with the walls of the container (Fig. 3.8).

The collision of gas molecules on the walls of the container exerts a force and this force acting per unit area gives the gas pressure.

Effect of Temperature on Pressure

When the temperature of a gas is increased, the molecules start moving with more and more velocity and hence, the number of collisions of the molecules on a given area on the walls of the container in a given time increases.

Moreover, since the velocity of the gas molecules increases, the kinetic energy of the molecules also increases. This in turn increases the impact of collisions of the molecules and hence, increases the pressure.

Effect of Volume on Pressure

Unlike solids and liquids, there is a lot of space between the molecules of a gas. Consequently, a gas can be compressed or expanded to a high extent. Pressure exerted by a gas depends on the volume of the gas. If the volume of the gas is increased, the space between the molecules increases. This reduces the number of collisions and hence the force per unit area on the walls of the container, thus reducing the pressure.

When a gas is compressed, the volume decreases and hence, the number of collisions increases. This increases the pressure.

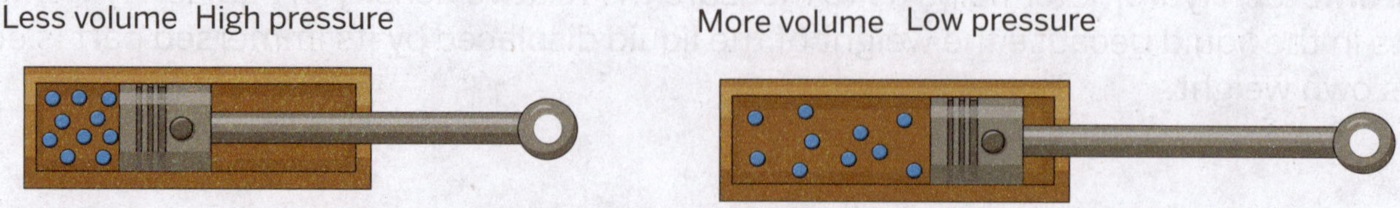

▲ Fig. 3.9 Pressure exerted by a gas depends on the volume of the gas

Atmospheric Pressure

The envelope of air around Earth is called the atmosphere. The height of the atmosphere extends up to a few kilometres from the surface of Earth. The pressure exerted by the atmosphere on the surface of Earth is called **atmospheric pressure**.

Atmospheric pressure is measured using a device called **barometer**. There are different types of barometers. Some of them are mercury barometer, aneroid barometer, water-based barometer and vacuum pump oil barometer.

Mercury Barometer

In 1643, Italian physicist Evangelista Torricelli invented this simple barometer to measure atmospheric pressure.

Mercury barometer (Fig. 3.10) consists of a long, glass tube of length 84 cm or more with one end closed and the other end open. The glass tube is filled with mercury and the open end is immersed in a trough containing mercury. A vacuum is created at the top end of the glass tube (closed end) as some mercury flows out of the tube to the trough.

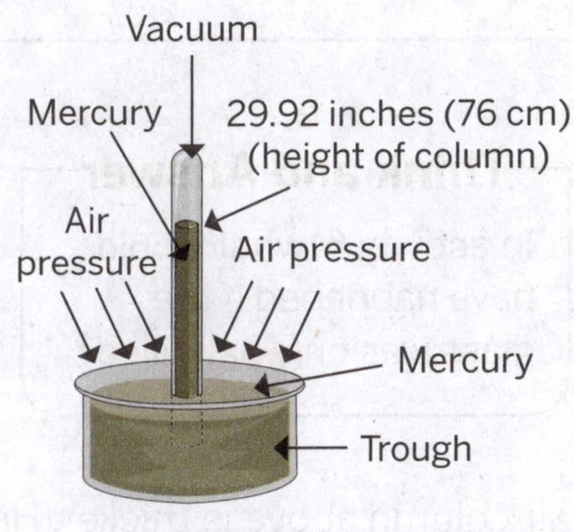

▲ Fig. 3.10 Mercury barometer

The level of mercury in the column gives the measure of the atmospheric pressure. The mercury level inside the glass tube gets adjusted until the pressure exerted by the weight of the mercury column balances the atmospheric pressure.

The vacuum created at the top of the glass tube is called **Torricelli's vacuum**. The length of the mercury column in the glass tube is 76 cm or 29.92 inches, when placed at sea level.

Effects of Atmospheric Pressure

Atmospheric pressure plays an important role in many of our day-to-day activities. When we drink something from a bowl or glass using a straw, the liquid rises through the straw due to the atmospheric pressure acting on the liquid in the bowl or glass. When we suck the liquid upwards, the pressure inside the straw decreases and the atmospheric pressure acting on the liquid in the bowl causes it to rise up through the straw.

When a rubber sucker is pressed on to a smooth surface, the air between the sucker and the surface escapes. The pressure inside the rubber sucker becomes less than the atmospheric pressure (pressure of the air from outside) acting on it. Therefore, we find it difficult to remove it as the greater atmospheric pressure pushes it from outside.

▲ Fig. 3.11 Effects of atmospheric pressure

Activity 6

Aim: To show the presence of atmospheric pressure

Materials required: Cardboard, glass and water

Procedure:

1. Fill the glass with water up to the brim. Cover the glass with a cardboard and press slightly.
2. Turn over the glass quickly so that it is placed upside down on the palm of your hand.
3. Remove your hand slowly from the cardboard.

Observation: Even when you remove your hand, the cardboard remains stuck to the glass and does not fall out spilling the water.

Conclusion: The cardboard is supported by the atmospheric pressure acting from outside.

Think and Answer

In activity 6, what would have happened if the glass was only half filled?

Atmospheric Pressure Varies With Altitude

The altitude is the height of a place from sea level. As we go higher up, the altitude increases. With an increase in altitude, the atmospheric pressure decreases because the layer of the air column above us becomes thinner. Hence, the pressure exerted by the air on us decreases. This means that the atmospheric pressure at sea level is higher as the layer of the air column above is thicker. Hence, the pressure exerted by air is more at a lower altitude. But this high atmospheric pressure does not affect us because fluids such as blood in our body also exert a pressure, which balances the effect of atmospheric pressure.

Science in Context

Mountaineers carry oxygen cylinders with them because the low atmospheric pressure at the top of the mountains might cause nose bleeding. Moreover, the availability of oxygen is also less as we go to higher altitudes.

Lift Pump

Lift pump is a device used to take water from a lower ground level to a higher level. It works on the effect of atmospheric pressure.

A lift pump consists of a cylinder with a movable piston. There are two valves A and B, which open and close as the piston moves up and down. The steps involved in the working of a lift pump are shown in Fig. 3.12.

1. When the handle is raised, the piston moves down. As the piston moves down, valve A closes and valve B opens and therefore, the air inside the cylinder escapes through valve B.

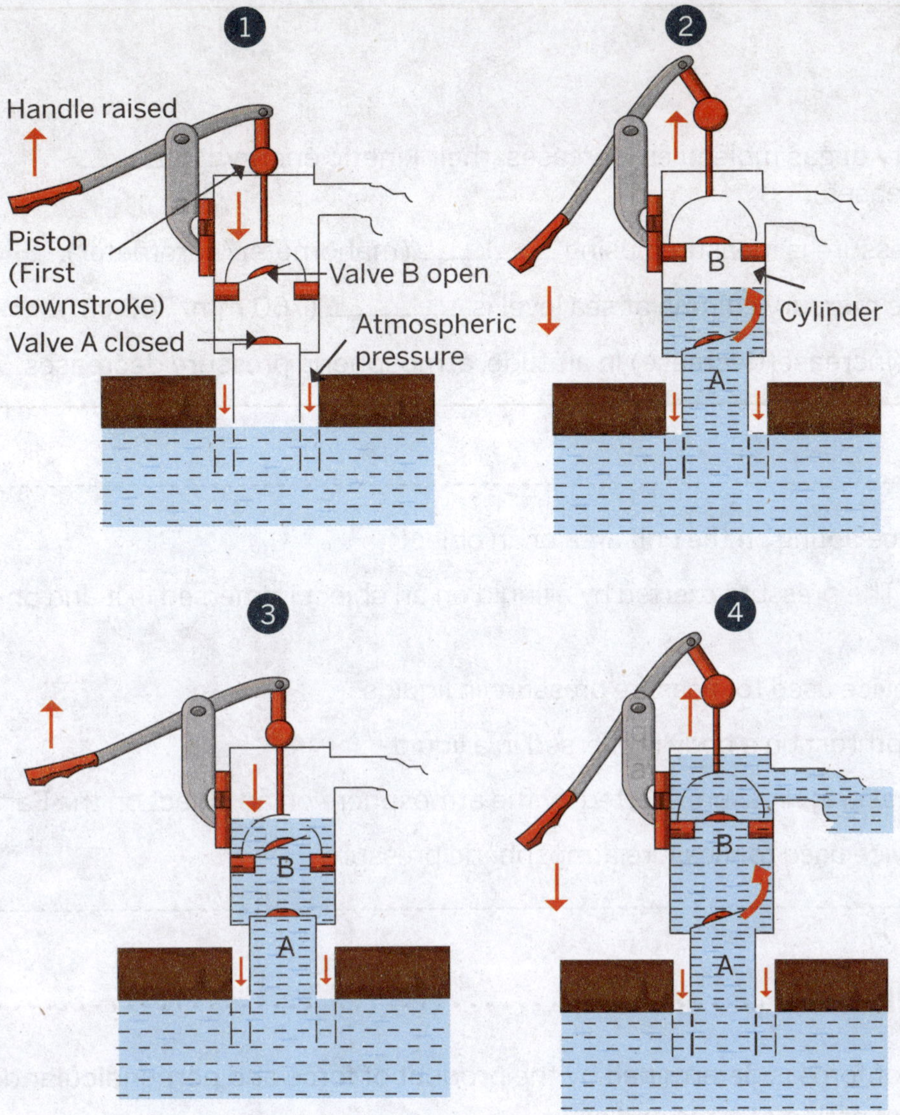

▲ Fig. 3.12 Working of a lift pump

2. When the handle is lowered, the piston moves up. As the piston moves up, valve A opens and valve B closes. The pressure inside the cylinder decreases after the air has escaped from it. So, the pressure acting on the water pushes it up through valve A and the water rises to the cylinder.
3. When the handle is raised again, the piston moves down and hence, the valve A closes and valve B opens. This releases the water in the cylinder through valve B and the outlet.
4. The repeated up and down movement of the handle of the lift pump helps to lift the water continuously.

Revision Zone

Fill in the blanks.

1. When the velocity of gas molecules increases, their kinetic energy ________ (increases/decreases).
2. Atmospheric pressure is measured using ________ (manometer/barometer).
3. The length of the mercury column at sea level is ________ (760 mm/760 cm).
4. With ________ (increase/decrease) in altitude, atmospheric pressure decreases.

Keywords

Pressure: The force acting on the unit area of an object

Liquid pressure: The pressure exerted by a liquid on an object immersed in it and on the walls of the container

Manometer: A device used to measure pressure in liquids

Buoyancy: The upthrust on a body immersed in a liquid

Atmospheric pressure: Pressure exerted by the atmosphere on an object on the Earth

Barometer: A device used to measure atmospheric pressure

In a Nutshell

- The moment of force is determined by the product of force and perpendicular distance between line of action of force and pivot.
- The pressure exerted by a liquid depends on the height of the liquid and the density of the liquid.
- The SI unit of pressure is pascal(Pa).
- According to Archimedes' principle, the apparent weight loss of an object immersed in a liquid is equal to the weight of the liquid displaced by the object.
- Liquid pressure increases with depth.
- Atmospheric pressure decreases with altitude.

Exercise

1 Choose the correct answer for each of the following.

a. Which among the following is the correct unit of moment?

i. m ii. Nm
iii. N/m iv. N

b. Which of the following changes increase the moment of force on an object?

i. Increase distance between force and pivot
ii. Reduce distance between force and pivot
iii. Reduce magnitude of force
iv. Remove the pivot

c. The straps of a school bag are made broad to increase

i volume ii. force
iii. pressure iv. surface area

d. If the surface area on which a force acts is small, the pressure exerted is

i. more ii. less
iii. equal iv. None of these

e. As the altitude increases, atmospheric pressure

i. increases ii. decreases
iii. first increases and then decreases
iv. first decreases and then increases

f. Which of the following is used to measure atmospheric pressure?

i. Manometer ii. Barometer
iii. Thermometer
iv. Sphygmomanometer

g. The law of flotation is explained by

i. Pascal's principle
ii. Archimedes' principle
iii. Newton's law of gravitation
iv. Bernoulli's principle

2 Fill in the blanks.

a. The turning effect of a force is called ____________.(moment/ pressure)

b. A point about which an object can run is called ____________. (pivot/ force)

c. As we go to higher altitudes, the atmospheric pressure ____________. (increases/ decreases)

d. It is difficult to cut an object using a ____________ knife. (sharp-edged/blunt)

e. Liquids exert pressure in ____________. (downward direction only/all directions)

f. We are able to drink juice using a straw because of ____________ pressure. (fluid/atmospheric)

g. Pressure exerted by liquid depends upon the ____________ (size of particle/density of liquid).

h. SI unit of pressure is ____________ (newton/pascal).

3 Write T for True and F for False.

a. Pressure is the force acting on unit area of a surface.

b. The SI unit for moment is Nm.

c. Gases exert pressure in all directions.

d. Pressure exerted by a liquid depends on its density.

e. All liquids exert equal pressure at all points at the same depth.

f. The upward force exerted by a liquid on a body immersed in it is equal to the weight of the body.

❹ Match the following.

a.	Fluids	i.	Atmospheric pressure
b.	Manometer	ii.	Buoyant force
c.	Barometer	iii.	Liquids and Gases
d.	Archimedes' principle	iv.	Pressure exerted by liquids

❺ Define the following.

a. One pascal
b. Barometer
c. Pressure
d. Atmospheric pressure
e. Buoyant force

❻ Answer the following questions in brief.

a. Dams are made thicker at the bottom than at the top. Why?
b. What is the relation between pressure, force and area?
c. What is the cause of atmospheric pressure?
d. Mention two situations in our life where atmospheric pressure is helpful.
e. Explain Archimedes' principle.
f. State the condition for an object to float on the surface of a liquid.
g. What is buoyant force?

❼ Answer the following questions in detail.

a. Write any four applications of pressure.
b. A carton box exerts a pressure of 60 Pa on a table. Calculate the area of the table if the force exerted by the box is 120 N?
c. Define pressure. Mention any two situations where more pressure is helpful.
d. What is liquid pressure? Mention the properties of pressure exerted by liquids.
e. Explain one activity to demonstrate that liquid exerts pressure in all directions.
f. Discuss some applications of Archimedes' principle.
g. Explain the effect of volume on gas pressure.

❽ Solve the following numerical problems.

a. A force of 20 N is applied at a perpendicular distance of 4 m from a pivot. What is the moment?
b. A force of 1000 N is applied about an axis. If the length of the lever which connects the axis and the point of application of force is 1 m, what is the moment?
c. An elephant having a mass of 300 kg, is standing on a concrete bridge of length 8 m and breadth 4 m. Calculate the pressure exerted by the elephant on the bridge. Given, acceleration due to gravity is 9.8 m/s^2.
d. A hydraulic jack is used to lift a car of mass 1032 kg. The lift piston has a radius of 25 cm. What is the pressure exerted on the piston? Given, acceleration due to gravity is 9.8 m/s^2.
e. A swimming pool has a length of 30 m and a breadth of 10 m. Water is filled in the tank up to a height of 5 m. What is the pressure at the bottom of the pool due to the water? Given, density of water is 1000 kg/m^3 and $g = 9.8 \text{ m/s}^2$.
f. A cube of sides 5 cm is immersed in water. What is the difference in pressure at the bottom and top faces of the cube? Given, the depth of the top face from the water surface is 10 cm, density of water is 1000 kg/m^3 and $g = 9.8 \text{ m/s}^2$.

❾ Think and answer.

It takes more time to cook food on a mountaintop than at sea level. Explain.

❿ Project

Make a chart on various instruments used to measure pressure, for example, blood pressure, liquid pressure, atmospheric pressure. Collect their pictures, paste them on the chart and write a few lines on them.

Worksheet

A Subject Integration

Draw a graph against altitude and atmospheric pressure for the given data. Try to comprehend the atmospheric pressure for the geographical locations.

Altitude	Air Pressure
Sea Level	14.7 psi (101.3529 kPa)
10, 000 feet	10.5 psi (72.39495 kPa)
20,000 feet	6.2 psi (42.7475 kPa)
30,000 feet	4.1 psi (28.2685 kPa)
40,000 feet	2.5 psi (17.2369 kPa)
50,000 feet	1.3 psi (8.96318 kPa)

B Life Skills

Perform an activity to check atmospheric pressure. (This activity can be performed in a playground under the supervision of your teacher.)

Use the following materials for this activity.

Materials Required: Tub of water, Air pump, Gum.

Suppose you are playing football in a playground and your ball gets punctured. How will you find the area that gets punctured? You have to patch the ball and needs to fill the air to the ball to continue the game.

Hint: Relate the atmospheric pressure.

Energy

4

What I shall learn

- Work done
- Kinetic energy
- Potential Energy
- Energy transformation
- Power
- Energy conservation

Introduction

We perform a lot of physical and mental activities in our everyday life. Can we call these activities work? If we put effort (physical or mental), then we consider that as work. For example, reading a book, solving a maths problem, working on a computer, etc. However, in physics, all these activities are not considered as work.

In physics, work is said to be done only if a body undergoes a change in its position by a force. The following images show a few activities where work is done.

▲ Fig. 4.1 Situations where work is done

Remember

Force is a push or a pull acting on an object.

Work

Work is said to be done when a force displaces an object in the direction of the force. If there is no displacement of the body, then no work is said to be done. For example, a person holding a suitcase in his hand and standing does not do any work. However, a person lifting a suitcase from the ground does work as there is a pulling force applied to the suitcase in the upward direction and there is a change in position of the object. Hence, work is done in this case.

Let us look at another example. Consider two vegetable vendors: one selling in his shop and the other in his moving cart.

▲ Fig. 4.2 Vendor 1 and vendor 2

In both the cases, the vendors are selling vegetables. In the case of vendor 1, work is not being done as there is no displacement of objects, whereas in the case of vendor 2, work is being done as there is displacement of the cart with vegetables in the direction he pushes the cart.

Hence, for work to be done:

- There should be an applied force.
- The object on which force is applied should move due to the force.
- The direction of motion of the object should be along the direction of the force applied.

Work is not done when:

- The applied force does not displace the object.
- The displacement of the object is perpendicular to the direction of the applied force.
- The displacement of the object is not due to the force applied.

Challenge Yourself

We have learned that force can also stop a moving object, and change the size and shape of an object in addition to making an object move. Based on that, will there be any work done in the following cases.

- A goalkeeper stopping a football from entering the goal
- Squeezing a wet towel

Examples of work being done

- A person pushing a trolley in a supermarket: The trolley moves in the direction of the force (push) applied.
- A horse pulling a carriage: The carriage moves in the direction of the force applied.
- A person carrying a box on his head and climbing a staircase.
- A person lifting a box from the ground.

Examples of work not being done

- A child pushing a fixed wall: The wall cannot move due to the force applied by the child. Hence, displacement is zero and no work is done.

Challenge Yourself

Work is done when we lift an object from the ground. What about dropping an object to the ground?

> **Remember**
>
> Work is done on an object when:
> - we lift it up
> - we lower it
> - we speed it up
> - we slow it down

- A man standing with an object in his hand: No work is done on the object as there is no displacement of the object in the direction of the force, which is the gravitational force.
- A ball rolling on a smooth frictionless surface: The ball is moving without the application of any force. Since there is no applied force, no work is done. So, even though there is a displacement of the ball, no work is done on it.

Calculating Work Done

Work done is calculated as the product of force and displacement in the direction of the force.

Work done = Force × Displacement

Let F be the force applied on the object and S be the displacement of the object. Then,

$W = F \times S$

SI Unit of Work

SI unit of work is **joule** (J). Work done is the product of force and displacement. The SI unit of force is newton (N) and that of displacement is metre (m). Hence, the unit of work is newton metre (Nm). One newton metre is equal to one joule (J).

The amount of work done is said to be one joule if one newton force displaces a body through one metre in the direction of the force.

Solved Problems

1. A force of 10 N acting on an object displaces it through a distance of 10 m. Find the work done.

Solution:

Given, F = 10 N, S = 10 m

Work done, $W = F \times S$

So, $W = 10\text{ N} \times 10\text{ m} = 100\text{ Nm}$

$= 100\text{ J}$

2. The force applied by a bullock to pull a cart is 1000 N and the distance moved by the cart is 30 m. What would be the work done?

Solution:

Given, F = 1000 N and S = 30 m

Work done, $W = F \times S$

So, $W = 1000 \times 30 = 30{,}000\text{ Nm}$

$= 30{,}000\text{ J}$

3. Calculate the applied force on a body to move it by a distance of 2 m. The work done is 28 J.

Solution:

Given, W = 28 J = 28 Nm and S = 2 m

Work done, W = F × S

So, applied force, $F = \frac{W}{S}$

$F = \frac{28}{2} = 14$ N

4. Calculate the displacement of a ball if the work done is 320 J with a force of 16 N applied on it.

Solution:

Given, W = 320 J = 320 Nm and F = 16 N

Work done, W = F × S

So, displacement, $S = \frac{W}{F}$

$S = \frac{320}{16} = 20$ m

5. Calculate the work done by a boy in trying to push a tree with the applied force of 25 N.

Solution:

Given, F = 25 N

We know that, work done, W = F × S

In this case, it is obvious that there is no displacement as the boy is trying to push the tree. That is, S = 0.

Hence, W = 25 × 0 = 0

Challenge Yourself

What is the work done if a force of 8 N moves a body through a distance of 3 cm? Write the answer in the unit Nm (J).

Revision Zone

Solve the following numerical problems.

1. Calculate the force applied on a bike if it is moved 20 m and the work done is 400 J.
2. Calculate the work done by a wrestler to push a competitor 10 m away with a force of 800 N.

Energy

We have learned that energy is the capacity to do work. We need energy to do any kind of activity or work. For example, we need energy to walk, play, move an object, concentrate on studies, etc. Machines also require energy to do work. Therefore, all living and non-living things need energy for their functioning.

The unit of energy is same as work; that is, **joule** (J). This is because the energy supplied is utilized to do work.

Know the Scientist

The SI unit of energy and work, joule, is named in the honour of the English scientist, **James Prescott Joule**. He was the first to study the nature of heat and its relationship with mechanical energy, which eventually led to the law of conservation of energy.

Forms of Energy

We, human beings, get energy from the food we eat. When we run around and play for a long time, we use the stored energy in our body; hence, we get tired. We then have to consume food and water to regain energy.

Energy exists in many forms such as light energy, heat energy, sound energy, electrical energy, mechanical energy, etc. Some forms of energy are stored and can be used whenever needed. They get over after they are used for doing work. Some forms of energy are easily available for use such as light energy from the sun. Let us learn about kinetic energy and potential energy.

▲ Fig. 4.3 A moving car has mechanical energy

Mechanical Energy

Mechanical energy is the energy associated with either the motion or the position of an object. The energy possessed by an object by virtue of its motion is called **kinetic energy**. The energy possessed by an object by virtue of its position and location is called **potential energy**. The sum of kinetic energy and potential energy of a body gives its total mechanical energy.

Kinetic Energy

The energy possessed by a body by virtue of its motion is called kinetic energy. Kinetic energy of a moving object depends on the mass of the object and its speed in a given direction, which is known as **velocity**. Kinetic energy is given by the formula, $KE = \frac{1}{2}mv^2$, where m is the mass of the object and v is its velocity.

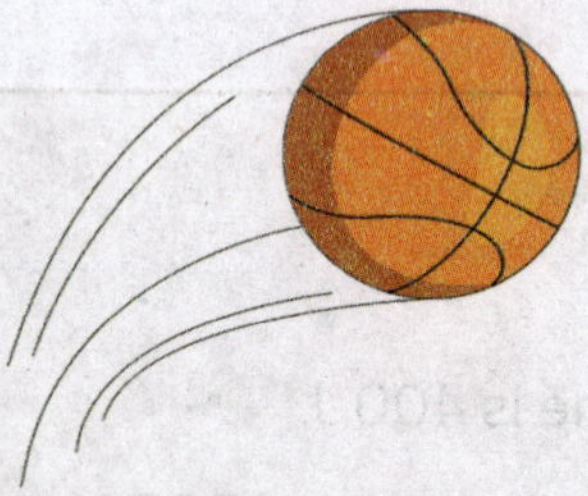

▲ Fig. 4.4 A moving body possess kinetic energy

Flowing water, a moving ball, a moving car, etc., are a few examples of things that possess kinetic energy. In many cases, kinetic energy is derived from the stored potential energy. For example, a stretched bow has potential energy stored in it. When released, this energy is transferred to the arrow as kinetic energy that results in its motion.

Potential Energy

Potential energy of an object is the energy that is stored in it. Water stored in a dam, a stretched rubber band, a stretched bow, a compressed or a stretched spring, etc., possess potential energy. Potential energy can be divided into two categories:

- Gravitational potential energy
- Elastic potential energy

▲ Fig. 4.5 Girl on the top of a slide has gravitational potential energy

Gravitational Potential Energy

It is the potential energy possessed by a body by virtue of its position. When an object is placed at a certain height from the ground, it possesses gravitational potential energy. For example, a girl sitting on the top of a slide has gravitational potential energy. Gravitational potential energy of an object of mass m at a height h is equal to the work done in lifting the object to that height.

The force required to lift an object from ground = weight of the object = mg

Work done in lifting the object to a height h is

W = force × displacement = $mg \times h$

So, gravitational potential energy = mgh

Gravitational potential energy increases with an increase in the height of the object from the ground.

▲ Fig. 4.6 A stretched bow has elastic potential energy

Elastic Potential Energy

It is the potential energy possessed by a body by virtue of its orientation. When an object is compressed or stretched or bent, the energy is stored in the form of elastic potential energy. A bow and arrow works on the mechanism of elastic potential energy. The amount of potential energy stored in the stretched bow determines the distance travelled by the arrow upon release. Similarly, a stretched wire, a stretched or compressed spring, etc., all possess elastic potential energy.

Remember

Speed is the distance travelled by a particle in unit time.
Velocity is the speed in a given direction.
Gravitational potential energy = mgh
Kinetic energy = $\frac{1}{2} mv^2$

Solved Problems

1. Calculate the potential energy of a stone which is kept at a height of 300 m, whose mass is 20 kg. Assume acceleration due to gravity as 10 m/s^2.

   Potential energy = mgh

   $m = 20 \text{ kg}, g = 10 \text{ m/s}^2, h = 300 \text{ m}$

   $mgh = 20 \times 10 \times 300$

   Therefore, potential energy = 60000 Nm

2. Calculate the kinetic energy of a roller coaster rolling down with a speed of 5 m/s. The mass of the roller coaster is 2000 kg.

   $KE = ½ mv^2 = \frac{1}{2} \times 2000 \times (5 \times 5) = 25000 \text{ J}$

Revision Zone

1. Mass of an object is 10 kg. The object is placed at a height of 50 m. Assume acceleration due to gravity as 10 m/s^2. Find potential energy of the object.
2. Calculate the kinetic energy of a ball rolling from the slope with a speed of 3 m/s. The mass of the ball is 200 g.

Energy Transformation

We have now learned about different forms of energy. Do you think they get created on their own? Will the various types of energy in the universe get over after we have used them for some time?

Energy can be neither created nor destroyed or exhausted. Energy can only be transformed from one form to another. This is known as the **law of conservation of energy**, which states that energy can neither be created nor be destroyed, but can be converted from one form to another.

Some of the energy conversions we come across in our day-to-day life are given below:

- When a stretched bow is released, potential energy of the bow is converted into kinetic energy of the arrow.
- A rock sitting at the edge of a cliff has potential energy. If the rock falls, the potential energy will be converted to kinetic energy.
- A ball thrown up has kinetic energy initially. As it goes upwards, the kinetic energy will be converted to potential energy.
- As a roller coaster goes up, it loses kinetic energy and gains potential energy. When it comes down it loses potential energy and gains kinetic energy.
- Water stored in a water tank possesses potential energy. When water is released it is converted to kinetic energy.

Power

The rate of doing work is called **power**. If W is the amount of work done in time T, then the power is given by the expression,

Power = Work/Time = Energy/Time

$P = W/T$

The SI unit of power is watt (W) which is equal to joule (J) per second.

A body is said to have power of 1 watt if it works at the rate of 1 joule in 1 second, i.e.,

1 W = 1 J/1 s

Table 4.1 given below shows the differences between energy and power.

Table 4.1 Difference between Energy and Power:

	Energy	Power
1.	Capacity to do work	Rate of doing work
2.	SI unit of energy is joule	SI unit of power is watt
3.	Energy can be transformed from one form to another	It measures the rate of energy transfer

Energy Conservation

We need to conserve sources of energy to prevent their scarcity in the future. Conserving energy helps us to minimize the usage of energy sources and thus, save our money. Following are some of the steps that need to be taken to conserve energy.

- Wherever possible, use solar-based appliances that save electricity to a large extent, for example, solar cookers and solar lamps.
- Switch off lights, fans and television when not in use. Using more than one television in a house can be avoided.
- Avoid overheating or overcooling while using water heaters and air conditioners respectively.
- Close the windows when the AC is switched on.
- Instead of using tube lights, compact fluorescent light (CFL) or LED lamps can be used. This saves electricity.
- When you have to travel short distances, avoid taking a car. Instead, walk or ride your bicycle.

Relation between Work and Energy

We learned that energy is the capacity to do work. Energy and work are interconvertible. When we do work, energy is converted into work. Similarly, the work done on a body is converted into its energy. This is called the **work–energy principle**, which states that the work done on a body or by a body is equal to the change in its kinetic energy.

That is, $W = KE_2 - KE_1$

where, W is the work done, KE_1 and KE_2 are the initial and final kinetic energies of the body.

Revision Zone

Write T for True and F for False.

1. Wind possesses potential energy.
2. An archer's bow with the string pulled back is an example for elastic potential energy.
3. Flowing water is an example of kinetic energy.
4. Roller coaster undergoes both change in potential and kinetic energy.

Keywords

Work: if a force applied on an object makes that object move along the direction of the force, work is said to be done

Energy: capacity to do work

Kinetic energy: energy possessed by a body by virtue of its motion

Potential energy: energy possessed by a body by virtue of its position or orientation

In a Nutshell

- Work is said to be done when a force acts on an object causing it to move through a certain distance.
- Gravitational potential energy can be calculated using the formula, PE = mgh.
- Kinetic energy can be calculated using the formula, KE = $\frac{1}{2}mv^2$.
- The law of conservation of energy states that energy can neither be created nor be destroyed. It is converted from one form to another.

Exercise

1 Choose the correct answer for each of the following.

a. Which among the following is the unit of work?

i. N ii. Nm

iii. m iv. N/m

b. What is the work done if a force of 10 N moves a body through a distance of 5 m?

i. 2 J ii. 10 J

iii. 5 J iv. 50 J

c. Kinetic energy __________ with the increase in the speed of the moving object.

i. increases ii. decreases

iii. remains the same iv. will be zero

d. Kinetic energy is calculated by the formula, KE = __________.

i. $\frac{1}{2}mv$ ii. $\frac{1}{2}vm^2$

iii. mv^2 iv. $\frac{1}{2}mv^2$

e. The formula to calculate work done is

i. W= F × S ii. W = F/S

iii. W= F + S iv. W = F – S

2 Write T for True and F for False.

a. Energy and work share the same unit, that is, joule.

b. Work is said to be done when a body does not undergo any displacement.

c. Energy possessed by an object by virtue of its motion is called potential energy.

d. Energy can neither be created nor be destroyed.

e. Using solar lamps helps in energy conservation.

3 Fill in the blanks.

a. Work done can be calculated by the formula, W = __________ (F × S/F + S).

b. Energy possessed by virtue of motion is called __________ (potential/kinetic) energy.

c. Potential energy can be calculated using the formula, PE = __________ (mgh/mgh^2).

d. A bullet coming out from a rifle is an example of __________ (potential/ kinetic) energy.

e. Power is calculated by the formula, P = __________ (work X time/ work/time)

f. Using __________ (incandescent/ compact fluorescent) light bulbs helps in the conservation of energy.

4 Match the following.

a. Pulling a trolley	i. Gravitational potential energy
b. Child pushing a fixed wall	ii. Elastic potential energy
c. Girl sitting on the top of a slide	iii. Work is done
d. Bow and arrow	iv. Work is not done

5 Define the following.

a. Work

b. One joule

c. Elastic Potential Energy

d. Kinetic energy

e. Potential Energy

6 Differentiate between the following.

a. Work done and no work done

b. Kinetic energy and potential energy

c. Gravitational potential energy and elastic potential energy

d. Energy and Work

7 Give reasons for the following.

a. Flowing water possesses kinetic energy.

b. Stored water possesses potential energy.

c. Suppose a boy is climbing staircase. In this case, whether work is done or not? State the reason for the same.

d. A boy is carrying a box on his head and standing; is he doing any work? Give reason.

8 Choose the odd one out. Give reasons for the choice.

a. Standing person, Running water, Moving car

b. Roller Coaster, Water stored in water tank, A Running horse.

c. Bow and Arrow, A stretched rubber band, A moving ball, A moving car

d. A person riding a bicycle, A boy pushing the fixed wall, A person carrying a bag while walking.

9 Solve the following numerical problems.

a. Calculate the work done by a cyclist cycling with a force of 100 N to cover a distance of 50 m.

b. Calculate S, if W = 140 J and F = 70 N.

c. Calculate the force applied by a weightlifter if he lifts the barbell to a distance of 4 m. Work done is 3200 J.

d. Calculate the force required to move an object by 5 m when work done is 20 J.

e. Calculate work done by a person who rows a boat with the applied force of 300 N. Distance travelled by the boat is 55 m.

f. Find the potential energy of a rock which weighs 300 N kept at a height of 500 m. Assume acceleration due to gravity as 10 m/s^2 (Weight = mass x acceleration due to gravity).

g. Mass of the stone is 10 kg. It rolls down with the velocity of 5 m/s from the top of the mountain. Find the kinetic energy of the stone.

10 Answer the following questions in one sentence each.

a. What would be the work done by a person holding a bucket of water standing in the same place?

b. What is the SI unit of work?

c. What is gravitational potential energy?

d. What is potential energy?

e. What is conservation of energy?

f. List a few examples of different applications of conservation of energy.

11 Answer the following questions in brief.

a. What is mechanical energy?

b. Explain gravitational potential energy.

c. What is elastic potential energy? Give an example of the same.

d. State the law of conservation of energy.

e. List any five examples of energy transformations.

⓬ Answer the following questions in detail.

a. Give some examples of work done and no work done.

b. Explain the conservation of energy involved in the production of hydroelectric power.

c. In what form is energy possessed by:

   i. Water stored in a water tank.

   ii. A raised bat

   iii. A running horse

   iv. A streched rubber band

   v. Bow and arrow

   vi. Roller coaster

d. In what ways can energy be conserved?

e. Explain the relation between work and energy.

⓭ Think and answer.

When a glass bowl is dropped from 10 cm height near the ground level, there is less chance of breakage. But when it is dropped from 1 m height, it breaks. What is the reason behind this?

(Hint: Relate potential energy and kinetic energy.)

⓮ In the Library

Collect details about how energy transformations are carried out in a thermal power plant.

⓯ Project

With diagram and numerical values, illustrate few examples for work done and no work done.

⓰ Topics for Further Research

We have learned about energy and work, and their basic concepts. Try to explore more about 'Work done by a spring force'.

Worksheet

Subject Integration

1. You might have heard about "Jack-in-the-box toy". Try to make a diagram of it illustrating the mechanism of elastic potential energy.

2. The following images represent either kinetic energy or potential energy. Identify them and write them in the space provided.

____

____

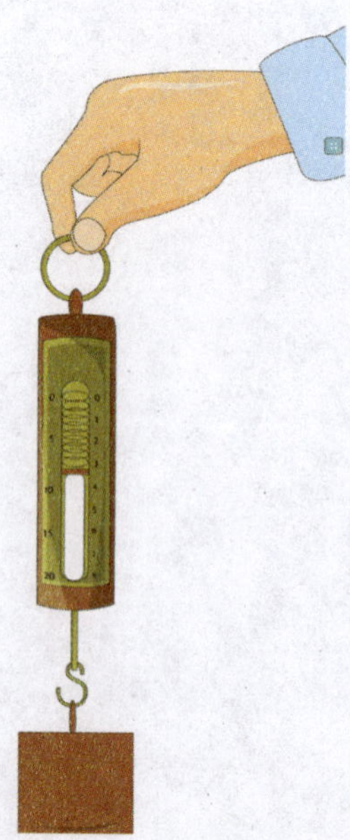

____

Light Energy: Curved Mirrors

5

What I shall learn

- Curved mirrors
- Image formation by a concave and convex mirror
- Real and virtual images
- Uses of curved mirrors

Introduction

A plane mirror has a plane reflecting surface. But there are mirrors that are not plane and have spherical or curved reflecting surfaces. Most of the kitchen utensils like steel vessels and spoons have curved reflecting surfaces. Take a polished steel spoon and look at both its surfaces. You will see an upright image at the back of the spoon and an inverted image on the hollow surface of the spoon.

These curved reflecting surfaces form curved or spherical mirrors. There are two kinds of curved or spherical surface—curved in and curved out. These two curves form two types of curved mirrors—concave and convex.

▲ Fig. 5.1 Images formed on the two sides of a spoon

Concave and Convex Mirrors

A **concave mirror** is a curved mirror whose reflecting surface is on the inner side. It is also known as a **converging mirror** as the parallel rays of light converge at a point after reflecting from the surface of a concave mirror.

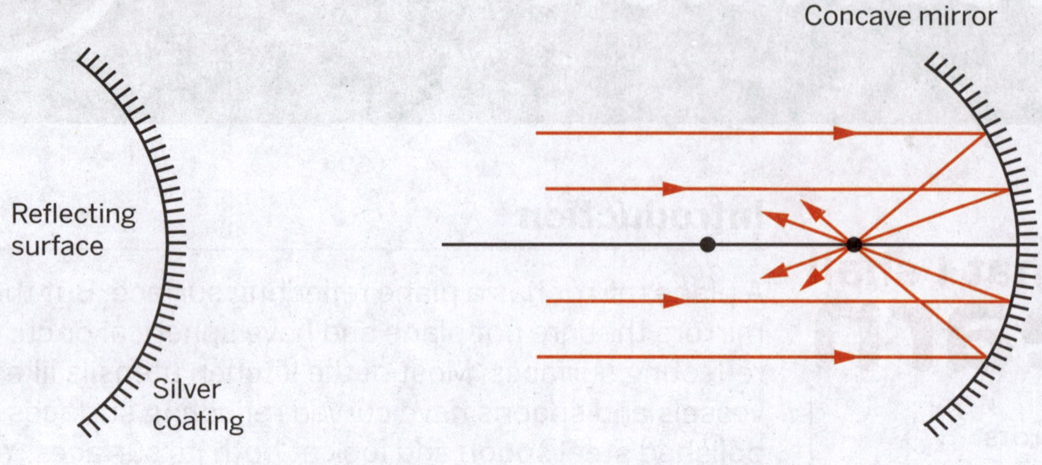

▲ Fig. 5.2 Representation of a concave mirror

A **convex mirror** is a curved mirror whose reflecting surface is on the outer side. It is also known as a **diverging mirror** as the parallel rays of light appear to diverge from a point after reflecting from the surface of a convex mirror.

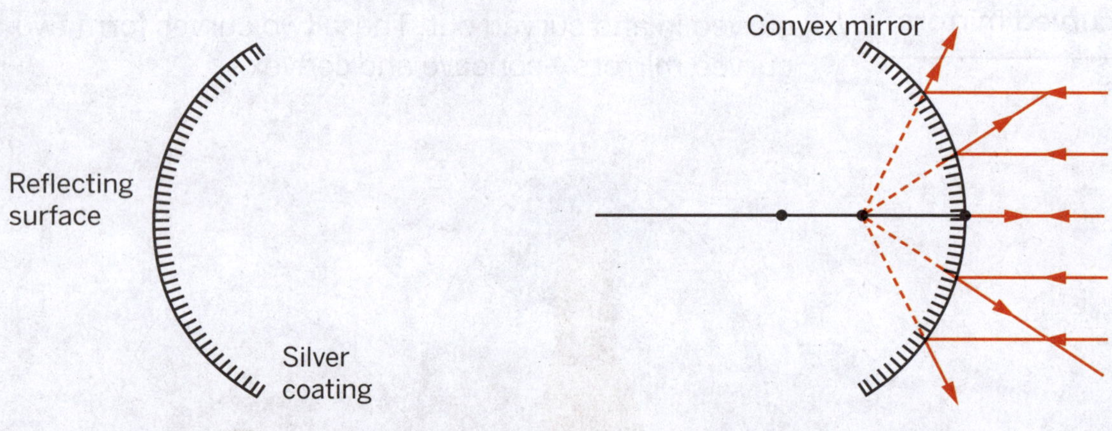

▲ Fig. 5.3 Representation of a convex mirror

Activity 1

Aim: To show that a parallel beam of light converges at a single point in front of the mirror after reflecting from a concave mirror

Materials required: Concave mirror and sheet of paper

Procedure: Hold the concave mirror in your hand so that the reflecting surface of the mirror faces the sun. Hold the paper in the other hand such that it faces the mirror. Adjust its position such that a clear single bright spot of light is formed on the paper. If we keep the mirror in this position for some time, we will notice that the paper will start burning.

Conclusion: A parallel beam of light after reflecting from a concave mirror converges at a single point.

Anatomy of Curved Mirrors

Curved mirrors—convex and concave—can be understood by the following terminologies:

1. Principal axis
2. Centre of curvature
3. Focal point/principal focus
4. Focal length
5. Radius of curvature

> **Remember**
>
> **Concave mirror**: Reflecting surface is on the inner side (curved in).
> **Convex mirror**: Reflecting surface is on the outer side (curved out).

Concave and convex mirrors can be considered as parts of a sphere. The line passing through the centre of the sphere to the exact centre of the mirror (known as vertex or pole, represented by P) is known as the **principal axis** of the mirror.

The centre of the sphere C is known as the **centre of curvature**. The point exactly in between the vertex and the centre of curvature is known as the **focal point** or **principal focus**. The focal point is denoted by the letter F and it is the point where the parallel rays of light converge or diverge after reflection. The distance between the vertex and focal point is known as **focal length** denoted by f. Radius of the sphere R is known as the **radius of curvature** of the mirror.

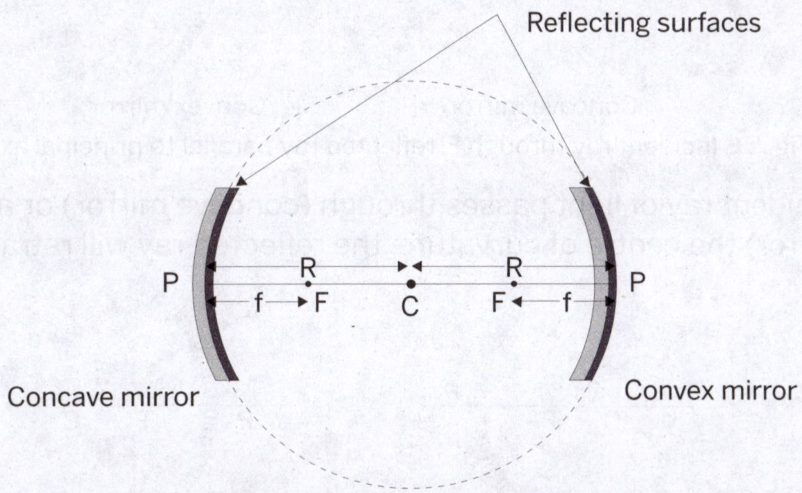

▲ Fig. 5.4 Anatomy of curved mirrors

Image Formation by a Concave and Convex Mirror

Due to the varying anatomy of convex and concave mirrors, the images formed by them differ. Let us understand them with the help of the ray diagrams.

Ray Diagrams

For a ray diagram to be drawn, we need a minimum of two reflected rays. In order to draw the images using ray diagrams we need to know the path of the incident rays and reflected rays. Let us discuss a few rules that give the paths of the incident and the reflected rays.

Case 1: When a ray of light is incident on a mirror such that it is parallel to the principal axis, the reflected ray will pass through the focal point of a concave mirror. The reflected ray from a convex mirror appears to be coming from the focal point after reflection.

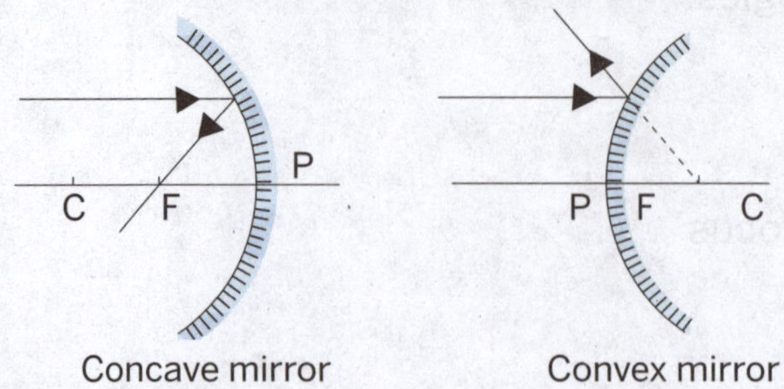

▲ Fig. 5.5 Incident ray parallel to principal axis, reflected ray through F

Case 2: When a ray of light is incident through the focal point of a concave mirror, the reflected ray will be parallel to the principal axis. For a convex mirror, when the incident ray appears to move in the direction towards the focal point, its reflected ray will be parallel to the principal axis.

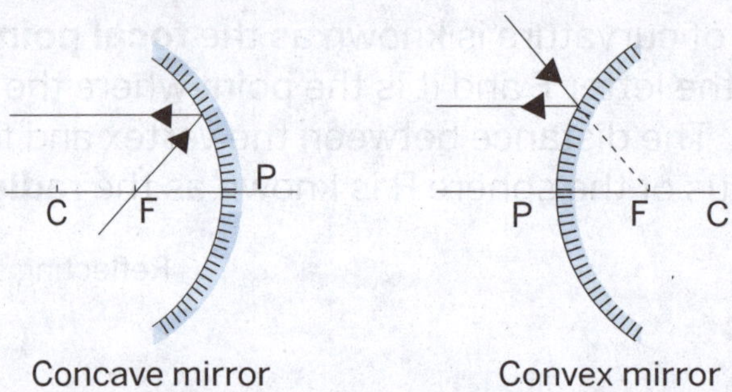

▲ Fig. 5.6 Incident ray through F, reflected ray parallel to principal axis

Case 3: When an incident ray of light passes through (concave mirror) or appears to pass through (convex mirror) the centre of curvature, the reflected ray will retrace the same path.

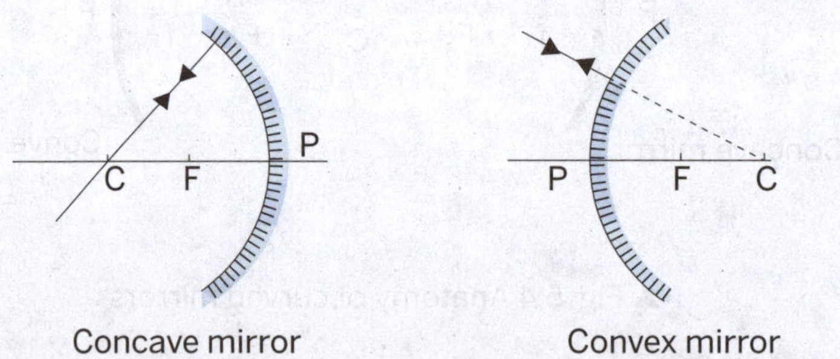

▲ Fig. 5.7 Incident ray and reflected ray through C

Case 4: When a ray of light is incident at the vertex P for the concave as well as the convex mirror, the angle of reflection will be equal to the angle of incidence.

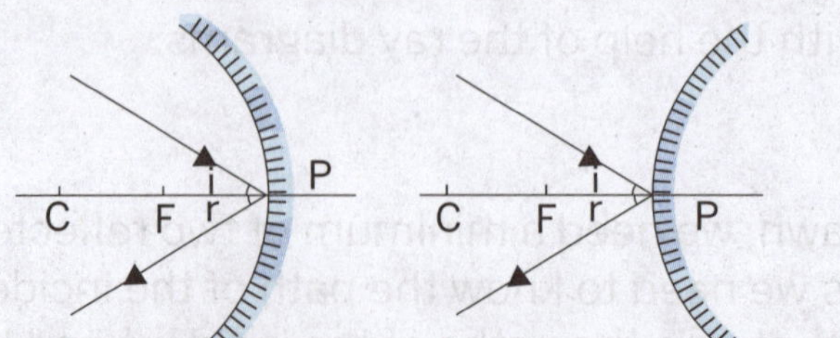

▲ Fig. 5.8 Incident ray at the vertex P

Image Formed by a Concave Mirror

Let us understand the image formed by a concave mirror when the object is placed at different positions.

1. **When the object is placed at infinity**: When the object is placed at infinity, the image will be formed at the focal point.

   Consider two rays: (a) a ray of light coming from infinity and reflecting at the vertex P and (b) a ray of light passing through the centre of curvature C and reflecting back along the same path. The image is formed at the intersection of the two reflected rays at F. The image formed will be real, inverted and diminished in size.

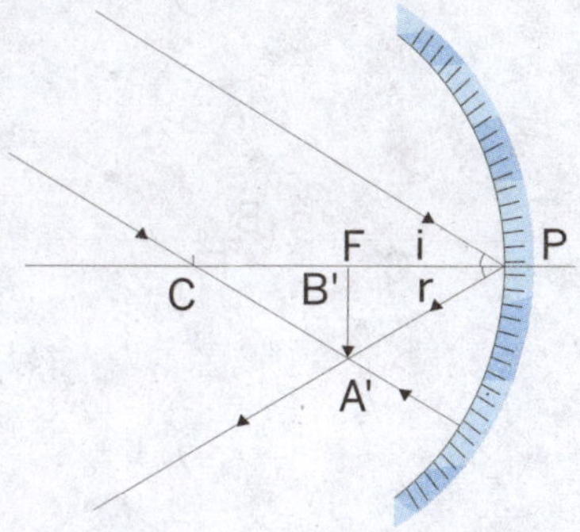

▲ Fig. 5.9 When object is placed at infinity

2. **When the object is placed beyond C**: When the object is placed beyond the centre of curvature, the image is formed in between the centre of curvature and the focal point.

   Consider two rays: (a) a ray of light from the object parallel to the principal axis which will be reflected through F and (b) a ray of light passing through the centre of curvature C and reflecting back along the same path. The image is formed at the intersection of the two reflected rays which is between F and C. The image formed will be real, inverted and diminished in size.

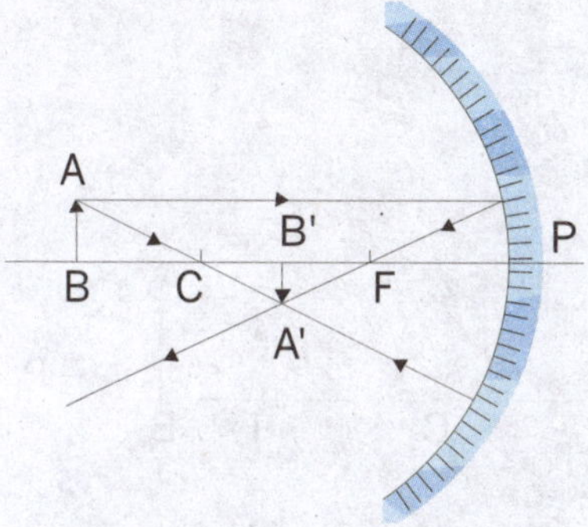

▲ Fig. 5.10 When object is placed beyond C

3. **When the object is placed at C**: When the object is placed at the centre of curvature C, the image will also be formed at the centre of curvature.

   Consider two rays: (a) a ray of light from the object parallel to the principal axis which will be reflected through F and (b) a ray of light incident through F which is reflected parallel to the principal axis. The image is formed at the intersection of the two reflected rays which is at C. The image formed will be real, inverted and of the same size as that of the object.

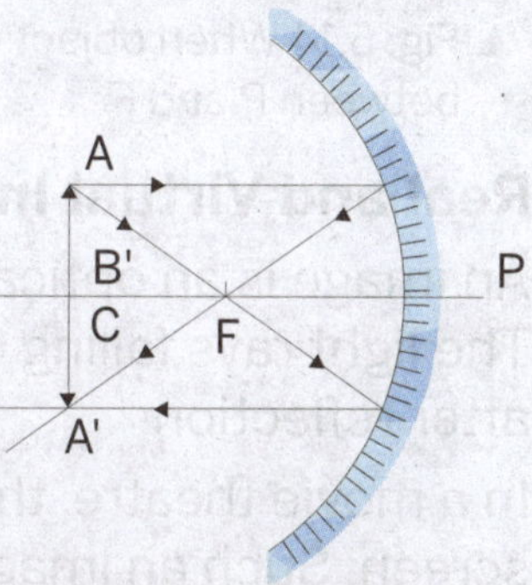

▲ Fig. 5.11 When object is placed at C

4. **When the object is placed between C and F**: When the object is placed in between the centre of curvature and the focal point, the image will be formed beyond the centre of curvature.

   Consider two rays: (a) a ray of light from the object parallel to the principal axis which will be reflected through F and (b) a ray of light incident through F which is reflected parallel to the principal axis. The image is formed at the intersection of the two reflected rays which is beyond C. The image formed will be real, inverted and enlarged.

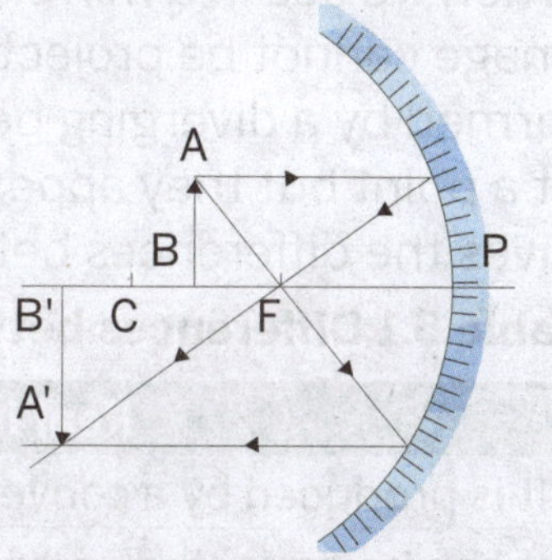

▲ Fig. 5.12 When object is placed between C and F

5. **When the object is placed at F**: When the object is placed at the focal point, the image will be formed at infinity

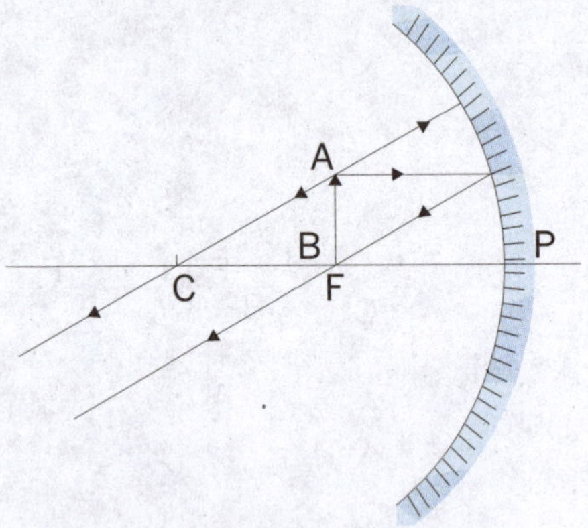

▲ Fig. 5.13 When object is placed at F

Consider two rays: (a) a ray of light from the object parallel to the principal axis which will be reflected through F and (b) a ray of light incident in a direction as though it is coming from the centre C and reflecting through C. The image is formed at the intersection of the two reflected rays. But the reflected rays are parallel and we assume that they intersect at infinity where the image will be formed. The image formed will be real, inverted and enlarged.

6. **When the object is placed between P and F**: When the object is placed in between the vertex P and the focal point F, the image will be formed behind the mirror.

Consider two rays: (a) a ray of light from the object parallel to the principal axis which will be reflected through F and (b) a ray of light incident in a direction as though it is coming from the centre C and reflecting through C. The reflected rays intersect at a point behind the mirror. The image is formed at the position from where the reflected rays appear to diverge. The image formed will be erect and enlarged. The image formed is virtual since it is appearing behind the mirror.

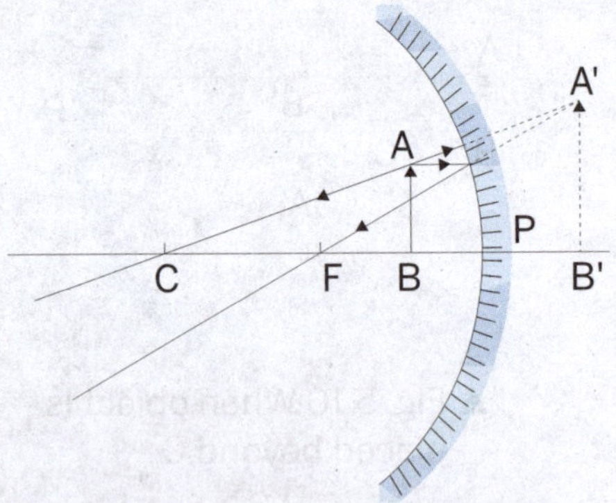

▲ Fig. 5.14 When object is placed between P and F

Thus, in all the cases, the image formed by a concave mirror is real except when the object is placed between the vertex P and the focal point. In this case, the image formed is virtual.

Real and Virtual Images

An image is an optical representation of an object. An image can either be real or virtual. The light rays falling on a mirror can converge at a point or appear to diverge from a point after reflection.

In a movie theatre, the light from a projector falls on a screen and an image is formed on the screen. Such an image is called a real image. Thus, an image formed by a converging beam of light is called a **real image**. Here, the light rays actually meet at a point to form the image.

When we see in a mirror, we see our image. Can this image be projected on a screen? This image cannot be projected on a screen and hence, it is called a virtual image. Thus, an image formed by a diverging beam of light is called a **virtual image**. Here, the light rays do not meet at a point but they appear to diverge from a point where the virtual image is formed. Table 5.1 gives the differences between real and virtual images.

Table 5.1 Differences between real image and virtual image

Real image	Virtual image
It is produced by a converging beam of light.	It is produced by a diverging beam of light.
It can be projected on a screen.	It cannot be projected on a screen.
It is always inverted.	It is always erect.

Image Formed by a Convex Mirror

Consider an object placed at any point in front of a convex mirror. To understand the size and orientation of the image formed by a convex mirror, let us consider two rays: (a) a ray of light from the object parallel to the principal axis whose reflected ray appears to come from the focal point F and (b) a ray of light incident in a direction towards the centre of curvature C and the reflected ray appears to come from C. The two reflected rays can be retraced back to a point behind the mirror. So, the image formed by a convex mirror is always a virtual image. The image will be erect (upright) and diminished in size.

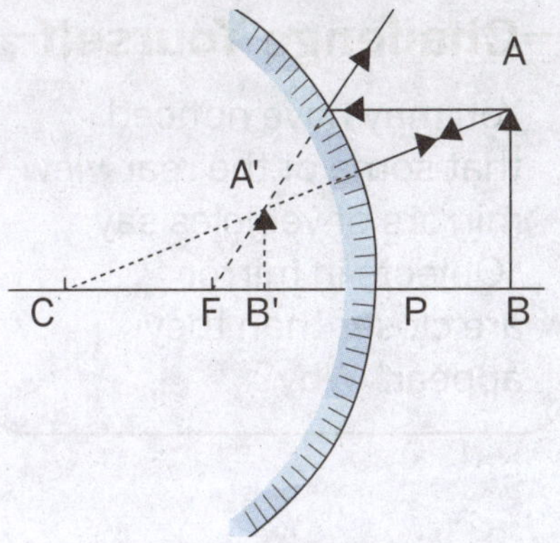

▲ Fig. 5.15 Image formation of a convex mirror

Activity 2

Aim: To demonstrate the formation of image by a concave mirror and a convex mirror

Materials required: Convex mirror, concave mirror, mirror stand, white screen and candle

Procedure: Light the candle and fix it on the table. Place a white screen near the candle, keep the concave mirror in front of the candle and the screen. Adjust the position of the mirror such that a clear image of the candle flame is formed on the screen.

1. Keep the mirror closer to the candle and adjust the position of the screen. What is the nature of the image?
2. Keep the mirror away from the candle and adjust the position of the screen. What is the nature of the image?
3. Move the mirror very close to the candle and adjust the position of the screen. Were you able to see the image on the screen? See the image in the mirror. What type of image were you able to see?

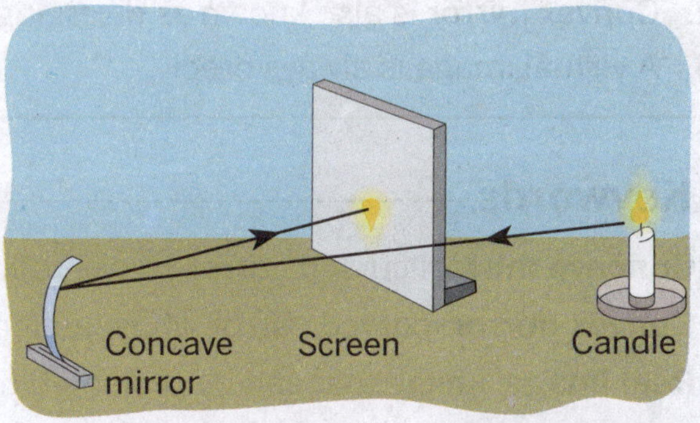

Now, repeat the same using the convex mirror. Was there any image formed on the screen? Observe the candle in the mirror by first placing it close to the candle and then away from the candle. What type of image is formed in each case?

Observation:

Mirror	Position of the Object	Nature of the Image		
Concave	Close to the mirror	Real	Inverted	Magnified
	Very close to the mirror	Virtual	Erect	Magnified
	Away from the mirror	Real	Inverted	Diminished
Convex	Close to the mirror	Virtual	Erect	Diminished
	Away from the mirror	Virtual	Erect	Diminished

In the case of convex mirror, no image is formed on the screen.

Challenge Yourself

You may have noticed that some of the rear-view mirrors of vehicles say: "Objects in mirror are closer than they appear." Why?

Uses of Curved Mirrors

- Concave mirrors with large focal length are used as shaving mirrors.
- Concave mirrors are used as reflectors in headlights of vehicles as they are more focused.
- Concave mirrors are used in search lights, flashlights, etc.
- Concave mirrors are used in devices like solar cookers, as they converge all the rays into one focused point.
- Concave mirrors are used in projectors as the output image is magnified.
- Concave and convex mirrors are used in reflection telescopes.
- Convex mirrors are used as rear-view mirrors of vehicles.
- Convex mirrors are used as field-view mirrors in supermarkets as they cover a wider range of vision.

Revision Zone

Write T for True and F for False.

1. Concave mirror is a curved mirror whose reflecting surface is on the outer side.
2. Convex mirror is also known as diverging mirror.
3. A virtual image is always erect.

Keywords

Concave mirror: curved mirror whose reflecting surface is on the inner side

Convex mirror: curved mirror whose reflecting surface is on the outer side

Real image: image that can be projected on a screen

Virtual image: image that cannot be projected on a screen

In a Nutshell

- A parallel beam of light converges at focal point after reflection from a concave mirror.
- A parallel beam of light appear to diverge from focal point after reflection from a convex mirror.
- The image formed by a concave mirror is real, in all the cases except when the object is placed between the vertex P and the focal point. In this case, the image formed is virtual.
- The image formed by a convex mirror is always a virtual image.

Exercise

1 Choose the correct answer for each of the following.

a. When a ray of light is incident on a concave mirror, the reflected ray will be
   i. divergent ii. parallel
   iii. convergent iv. none of these

b. The mirror that can form both real and virtual images is a
   i. convex mirror ii. concave mirror
   iii. plane mirror iv. all of these

c. Which mirror is used as the rear-view mirror of vehicles?
   i. Plane mirror ii. Concave mirror
   iii. Convex mirror iv. Cylindrical mirror

d. Which mirrors are used in projectors?
   i. Plane mirrors ii. Concave mirrors
   iii. Convex mirrors iv. Plano convex mirrors

2 Fill in the blanks.

a. A mirror that always forms an image of the same size as that of the object is a __________ (plane/concave) mirror.

b. An image that can be obtained on a screen is a __________ (real/virtual) image.

c. The distance between the vertex and the focal point is known as __________ (radius of curvature/focal length).

d. When a concave mirror is very close to the object, a __________ (real/virtual) image is formed.

e. When the object is placed beyond the centre of curvature, the image will be formed __________ (between C and F/at C).

3 Write T for True and F for False.

a. An erect image is always virtual.

b. A convex mirror can be used to obtain an enlarged and erect image of an object.

c. The erect image formed by a concave mirror can be obtained on a screen.

d. The beam of light after passing through a convex mirror will diverge.

e. Convex mirrors are used in search lights.

f. Concave mirror is also known as diverging mirror.

4 Define the following.

a. Principal axis of the mirror

b. Centre of curvature

c. Focal point/principal focus

d. Focal length

e. Radius of curvature

5 Differentiate between the following.

a. Real image and virtual image

b. Convex mirror and concave mirror

6 Name the following.

a. The image that cannot be obtained on a screen

b. The other name of the concave mirror

c. The mirror that forms only a diminished image

d. The direction of the reflected ray when a ray of light is incident through the centre of curvature

7 Answer the following questions in brief.

a. What is a focal point?

b. What do you mean by the principal focus of a convex lens?

c. What is the nature of image formed by a convex mirror?

d. Which mirror is used as a reflector in headlights of vehicles?

8 Answer the following questions in detail.

a. Draw a ray diagram to represent the image formed by a concave mirror when the object is kept between F and C.

b. Draw a ray diagram to represent the image formed by a concave mirror when the object is kept at F.

c. Draw a ray diagram to represent the image formed by a convex mirror when the object is kept in front of it.

d. Give any four uses of curved mirrors.

9 Think and answer.

The height of a real image formed by a concave mirror is 5 cm. The mirror is cut into two equal halves. What is the height of the image?

10 In the Library

Find out more information on the following topics:

- Reflection telescope
- Refraction of light

Worksheet

Write the nature of image (real/virtual; magnified/diminished/same size) that is formed in the cases shown below.

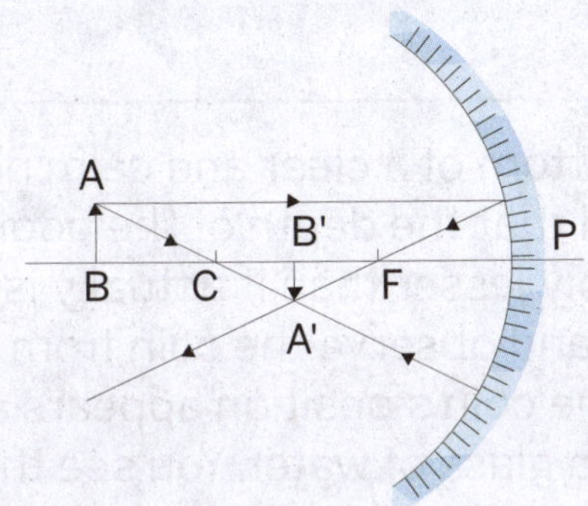

1. ______________

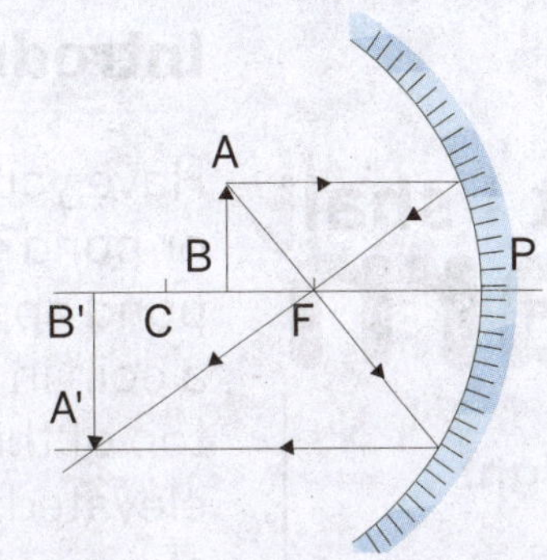

2. ______________

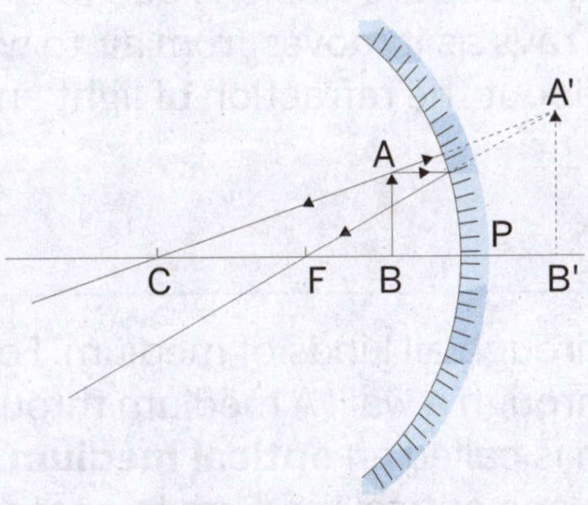

3. ______________

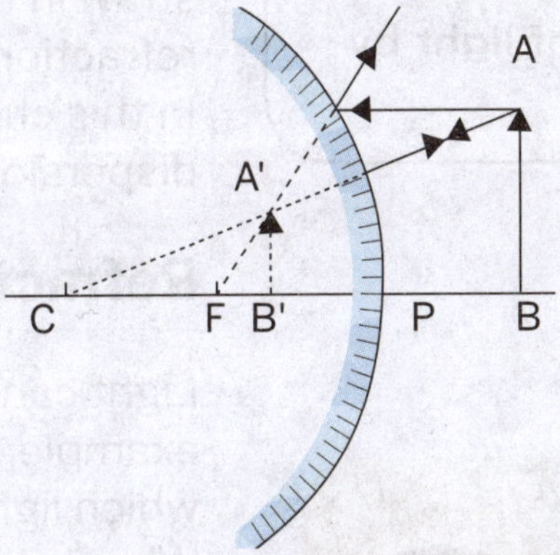

4. ______________

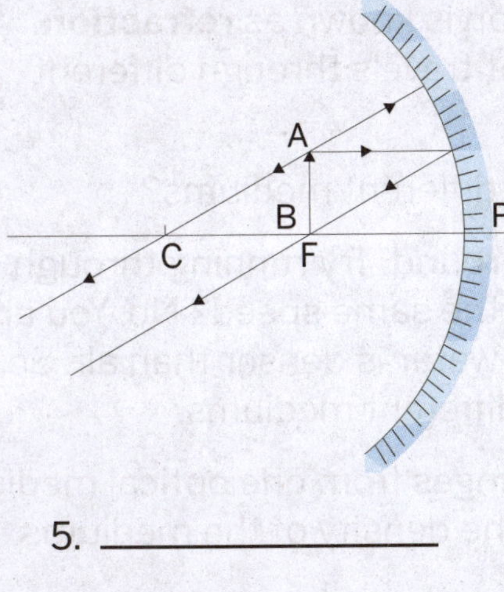

5. ______________

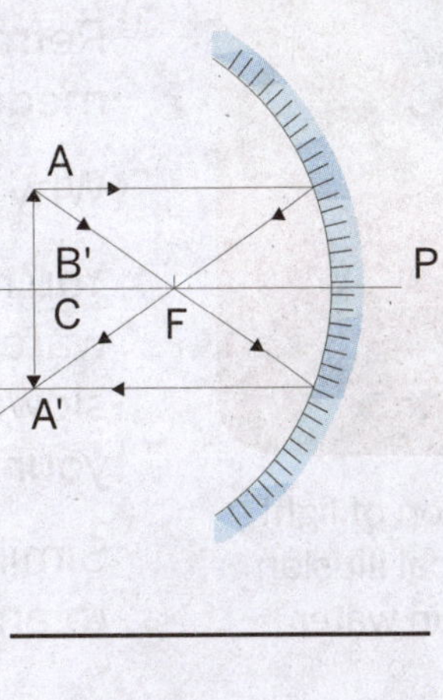

6. ______________

Light Energy: Refraction of Light

6

What I shall learn

- Refraction of light
- Bent effect due to refraction
- Refraction from a glass block and a prism
- Dispersion of light by a prism

Introduction

Have you ever looked at the bottom of a clear and calm pool or pond? You might have found that the depth of the pool or pond appears to be considerably lesser than it actually is. Put a coin in a glass of clear water and observe the coin from the top of the glass. You see that the coin's position appears a bit elevated. Now, keep a straw in a glass of water. You see that the straw appears bent from the point it touches the water.

We know that there is no change in the depth of the pool. The coin stays at the bottom of the glass. We also know that the straw in the water is not bent. These are illusions due to the refraction or bending of light rays as it moves from air to water. In this chapter, we will learn about the refraction of light and dispersion of light.

Refraction of Light

Light cannot travel or pass through all kinds of medium. For example, light cannot pass through a wall. A medium through which light rays pass through is called an **optical medium**. When a light ray passes from one optical medium to another optical medium of a different density, it deviates from its path by a certain angle at the surface of separation of the two mediums. This phenomenon is known as **refraction**. Refraction occurs because light travels through different mediums at different speeds.

▲ Fig. 6.1 Refraction of light creates an optical illusion of a bent straw in water

Why does the speed change in different mediums?

You run at a certain speed on ground. Try running through water in a pool. Can you run at the same speed? No. You are slowed down in water because water is denser than air. So, your speed will be different in different mediums.

Similarly, the speed of light changes from one optical medium to another due to a change in the density of the mediums.

Optically Denser and Rarer Mediums

Light travels at different speeds in different mediums which can be **denser** or **rarer** with respect to one another. These are relative terms that are used only when the densities of two mediums are compared.

- Light travels faster in a rarer medium than in a denser medium. A medium is said to be optically denser if it slows down the speed of light and it is said to be rarer if it increases the speed of light.
- Light travels fastest in vacuum where density is zero.
- Amongst the solid, liquid and gaseous states, the gaseous state is the rarest medium and the solid state is the densest medium.

Remember

A ray diagram is a diagram drawn using lines and arrows that traces the path of light.

Refraction Terminology

To understand the concept of refraction, let us consider a ray diagram as shown in Fig. 6.2.

- The ray (RO) which strikes the surface of separation of two optical medium is called the **incident ray**.
- The point on the surface of separation of the two medium where the incident ray strikes (O) is called the **point of incidence**.
- The straight line perpendicular to the surface of the medium and passing through the point of incidence is called the **normal**.
- The angle which an incident ray makes with the normal ($\angle i$) at the point of incidence is called the **angle of incidence**.
- From the point of incidence, the ray which changes its direction in the next medium (OR′) is called the **refracted ray**.
- The angle formed between a refracted ray and normal ($\angle r$) is called the **angle of refraction**.

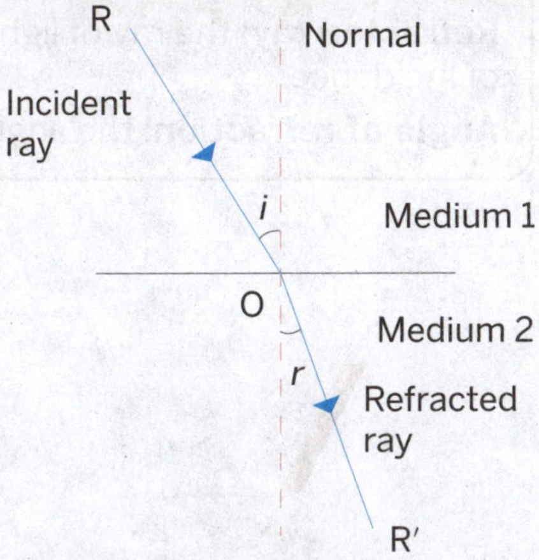

▲ Fig. 6.2 Refraction of light from medium 1 to medium 2

When light travels from a rarer medium to a denser medium, it bends towards the normal [Fig. 6.3 (a)]. This is because, in a denser medium, the ray of light tries to take the shortest route to exit the medium. In this case, the angle of refraction is less than the angle of incidence, ($\angle r < \angle i$). Denser the second medium, lesser will be the angle of refraction.

When light travels from a denser medium to a rarer medium, it bends away from the normal [Fig. 6.3 (b)]. In this case, the angle of refraction is greater than the angle of incidence, ($\angle r > \angle i$).

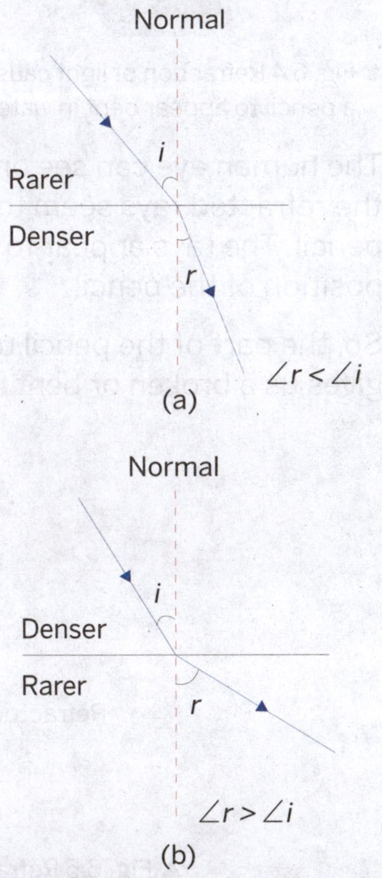

▲ Fig. 6.3 Refraction of light from (a) a rarer medium to a denser medium and (b) a denser medium to a rarer medium

Remember

Incident ray: the ray of light striking the surface of separation of the two mediums

Point of incidence: the point on the surface of separation of the two mediums where the incident ray falls

Normal: a straight line perpendicular to the surface of the medium and passing through the point of incidence

Angle of incidence: the angle between the incident ray and the normal

Refracted ray: the ray of light in the second medium after changing its direction at the point of incidence

Angle of refraction: the angle between the refracted ray and the normal

The Bent Effect Due to Refraction

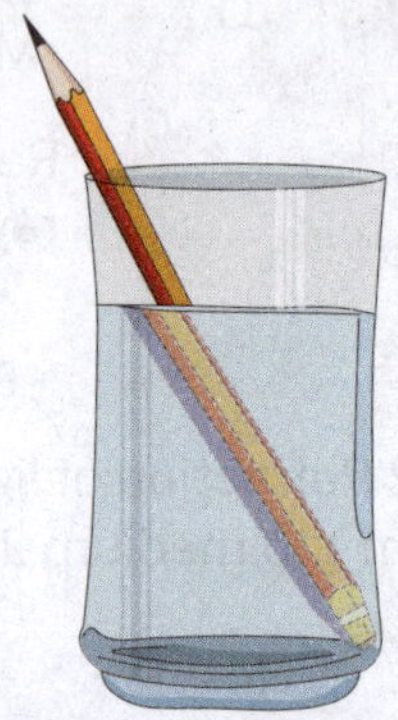

▲ Fig. 6.4 Refraction of light causes a pencil to appear bent in water

Consider a pencil dipped in a glass of water (Fig. 6.4). The pencil appears to be bent or broken. This is because water is denser than air. Let us understand how the bent effect occurs.

For us to see the pencil in the water, light must travel from the pencil through water, to air and finally to our eyes. A profile of the view of pencil (black dot) in water is shown in Fig. 6.5. As the light passes from water (denser medium) to air (rarer medium), it bends away from the normal. Bending of light at normal points M and N is shown in Fig. 6.5 (a).

The human eye can see only along the line of path of light that reaches the eye. In this case, the refracted rays seem to be coming from a point different from the actual position of the pencil. The rays appear to come from the grey coloured dot [Fig. 6.5 (b)] which is the apparent position of the pencil.

So, the part of the pencil under the water appears to have shifted towards one side, which gives us a broken or bent feel.

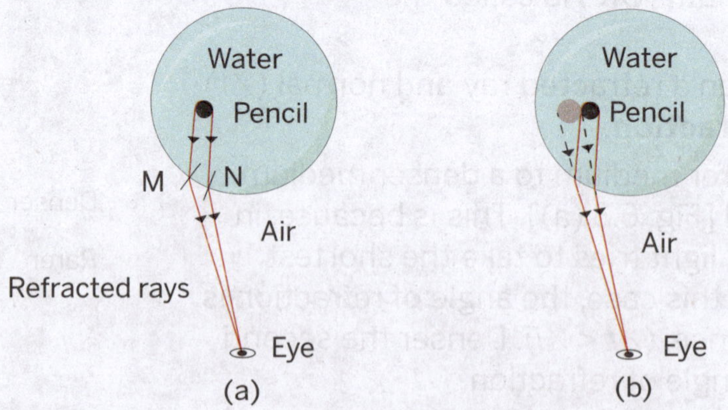

▲ Fig. 6.5 Refraction of light as it passes from water to air causes the bent effect

Let us understand the effect of refraction using some simple activities.

Activity 1

Aim: To understand the refraction of light

Materials required: Beaker, water and laser torch

Procedure:

1. Fill the beaker with water and keep it on a table.
2. Direct the light from the torch into the water from one side of the beaker, as shown in the image. Observe the path of light.

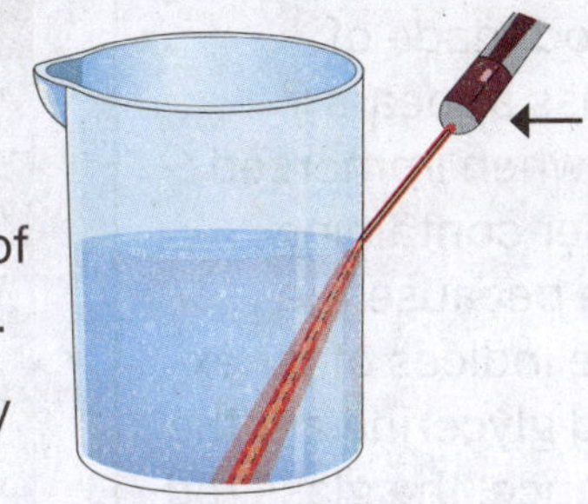

Observation: The light rays bend from their original path as they pass from air to water.

Conclusion: The light rays bend towards the normal (the side of the beaker from which the light enters the water) when they pass from air to water. This happens because water is optically denser than air.

Activity 2

Aim: To understand the refraction of light

Materials required: Bowl, coin and water (You require the help of a friend to perform this activity.)

Procedure:

1. Put the coin in the bowl.
2. While looking at the coin, move backwards till the coin becomes invisible to you.
3. Now, ask your friend to slowly pour water in the bowl. Observe what happens.

Observation: The coin becomes visible to you as the water gets filled.

Conclusion: When your friend pours water into the bowl, the light rays from the coin travel through the water first and then through the air. This change of medium causes the light rays to bend. When the light rays reach your eyes, the coin seems to be raised and becomes visible to you.

Refractive Index

The cause of refraction is the change in the speed of light as it moves from one medium to another. The refraction of light in a given medium can be expressed in terms of a factor called the **refractive index** of the medium. Refractive index of a medium is defined as the ratio of the speed of light in vacuum to the speed of light in the medium. It is also called the **index of refraction**. It is denoted by the Greek letter μ.

$$\text{Refractive index} = \frac{\text{Speed of light in vacuum}}{\text{Speed of light in the medium}}$$

that is, $\mu = \frac{c}{v}$.

where, c is the speed of light in vacuum and v is the speed of light in the medium. Slower the speed of light in a given medium, higher will be the refractive index and more will be refraction or bending of light towards the normal. Refractive indices of different substances/mediums are given in Table 6.1.

Science in Context

A glass rod made of pyrex glass appears invisible when immersed in a beaker containing glycerine because the refractive indices of pyrex glass and glycerine are the same. Hence, the glass rod appears invisible.

Table 6.1 Substances and their refractive indices

Substance/Medium	Refractive index
Vacuum	1
Air	1.003
Water	1.3
Oil, cedar	1.5
Diamond	2.4
Dense flint glass	1.6

If the refractive indices of two mediums are the same, then there will be no refraction of light rays when they pass from one medium to another.

Laws of Refraction

Let us look at the two laws of refraction.

First Law of Refraction

The first law of refraction states that the incident ray, the refracted ray, and the normal to the interface, all lie in the same plane.

Second Law of Refraction

The second law of refraction, also known as **Snell's law**, states that the ratio of the sine of the angle of incidence (sin *i*) to the sine of the angle of refraction (sin *r*) for any two mediums is always a constant. That is,

$$\frac{\sin i}{\sin r} = \text{Constant}$$

The value of this constant is the refractive index of the second medium with respect to that of the first. That is,

$$\frac{\sin i}{\sin r} = \text{Constant} = \frac{\mu_2}{\mu_1}$$

Consider a ray of light PO refracted at the interface of medium 1 and medium 2 as shown in Fig. 6.6.

Let $\angle i$ be the angle of incidence, $\angle r$ the angle of refraction, μ_1 the refractive index of medium 1 and μ_2 the refractive index of medium 2. Then,

$$\frac{\sin i}{\sin r} = \frac{\mu_2}{\mu_1}$$

We know that $\mu = \frac{c}{v}$.

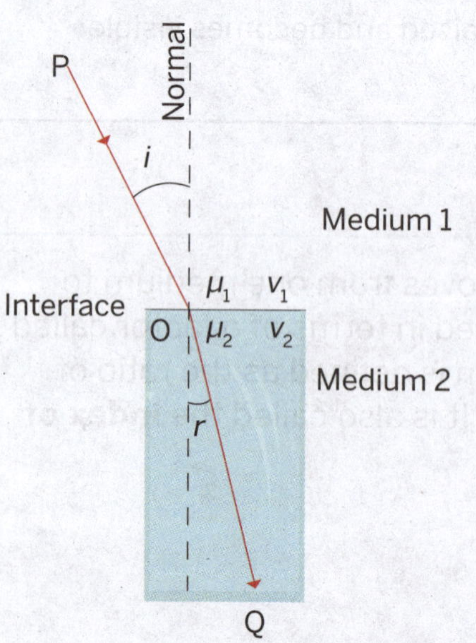

▲ Fig. 6.6 Refraction of light

So, if v_1 and v_2 are the velocities of light in medium 1 and medium 2 respectively, then

$$\mu_1 = \frac{c}{v_1} \text{ and } \mu_2 = \frac{c}{v_2}$$

So,

$$\frac{\sin i}{\sin r} = \frac{\mu_2}{\mu_1} = \frac{v_1}{v_2}$$

We consider the refractive index of vacuum as 1. So, speed of light in any medium can calculated as:

$$v = \frac{\text{Speed of light in vacuum}}{\text{Refractive index of the medium}}$$

Speed of Light in Water

Speed of light in vacuum $= 3 \times 10^8$ m/s

Refractive index of water $= 1.3$

So, speed of light in water $= \frac{3 \times 10^8}{1.3} = 2.3 \times 10^8$ m/s

Revision Zone

Fill in the blanks.

1. Light travels faster in a ______________ (denser/rarer) medium.
2. The denser the medium, the ______________ (more/lesser) will be the angle of refraction.
3. ______________ (Angle of refraction/Refractive index) is the ratio of the speed of light in vacuum to the speed of light in a medium.
4. Refractive index of water is ______________ (1/1.3).

Refraction Through a Glass Block

When a ray of light passes through a parallel-sided glass block, it bends towards the normal as it enters the block and away from the normal as it emerges from the block.

The refraction process is as follows.

1. When the ray of light passes from air to glass, it bends towards the normal N at the first interface. Let $\angle i$ be the angle of incidence and $\angle r$ be the angle of refraction.
2. As the refracted ray passes through the glass and exits from the second interface, it bends away from the normal N′. Let $\angle \Theta_1$ be the angle of incidence and $\angle \Theta_2$ be the angle of refraction at the second interface.
3. Let μ_1 be the refractive index of air and μ_2 the refractive index of glass. From Snell's law, we have for the refraction at the first interface:

$$\frac{\sin i}{\sin r} = \frac{\mu_2}{\mu_1}$$

For refraction at the second interface,

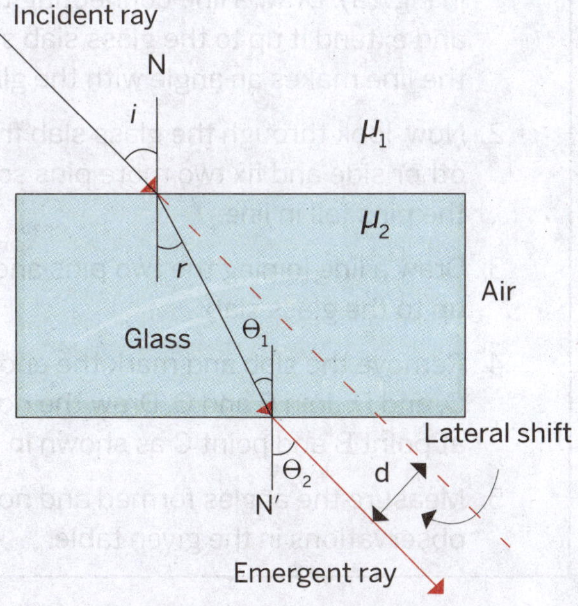

▲ Fig. 6.7 Refraction of light in a parallel-sided glass block

$$\frac{\sin \Theta_1}{\sin \Theta_2} = \frac{\mu_1}{\mu_2}$$

which means that

$$\frac{\sin i}{\sin r} = \frac{\sin \Theta_2}{\sin \Theta_1}$$

Since, the opposite sides of the glass slab are parallel, from the geometry of angles, we can see that $\angle\Theta_1 = \angle r$.

So, $\frac{\sin i}{\sin r} = \frac{\sin \Theta_2}{\sin r}$ which gives, $\angle\Theta_2 = \angle i$.

That is, the angle of emergence is the same as the angle of incidence.

4. The ray of light that leaves the glass slab is parallel to the ray of light that enters it.

As seen from Fig. 6.7, the ray of light emerging from the glass slab after two refractions shifts by a distance *d* from the original direction of the ray of light. This perpendicular distance between the emergent ray and the incident ray is defined as **lateral shift**.

Let us perform a simple activity to understand the refraction of light through a glass block.

Activity 3

Aim: To observe the refraction of a narrow beam of light through a parallel-sided glass block

Materials required: Glass slab, ball pins, white paper, cardboard and protractor

Procedure:

1. Place the glass slab on a white sheet (over a cardboard) and mark its outline. Fix the two pins on one side of the white paper as shown in Fig. (a). Draw a line connecting the two pins and extend it up to the glass slab such that the line makes an angle with the glass slab.
2. Now, look through the glass slab from the other side and fix two more pins so that all the pins fall in line.
3. Draw a line joining the two pins and extend it up to the glass slab.
4. Remove the slab and mark the ends as A, B, C, and D. Join B and C. Draw the normal each at point B and point C as shown in Fig. (b).
5. Measure the angles formed and note your observations in the given table.

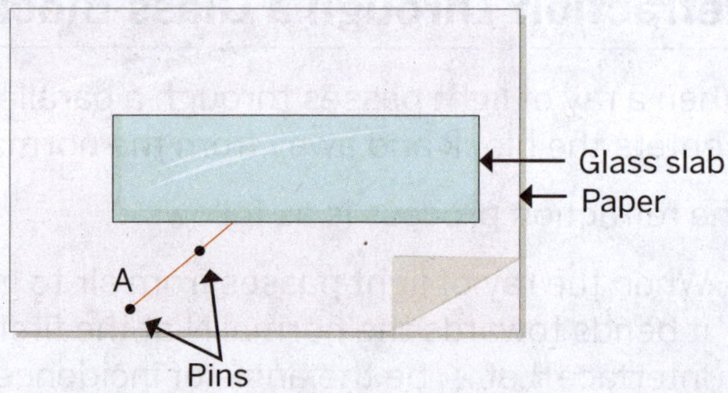

(a)

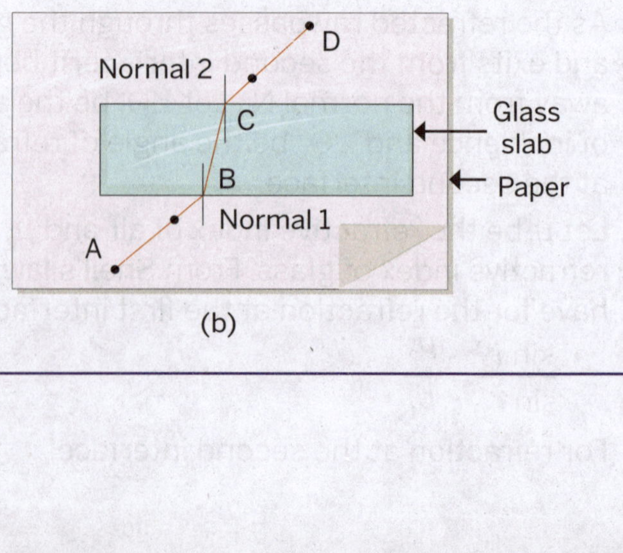

(b)

Observation:

Angle between AB and Normal 1 ($\angle i_1$)	Angle between BC and Normal 1 ($\angle r_1$)

Angle between BC and Normal 2 ($\angle i_2$)	Angle between CD and Normal 2 ($\angle r_2$)

Conclusion: The angle of incidence ($\angle i_1$) and the angle of emergence ($\angle r_2$) are the same. So, the emergent ray is parallel to the incident ray.

To understand lateral shift, let us do the following activity.

Activity 4

Aim: To understand lateral shift due to refraction

Materials required: Glass slab and three pens

Procedure: Line up the pens on a table and place the glass slab on them. Observe the pens through the glass slab.

Observation and conclusion: The position of the pens appears to have shifted under the slab. This occurs because of the lateral shift of the emergent rays from the glass slab after refraction.

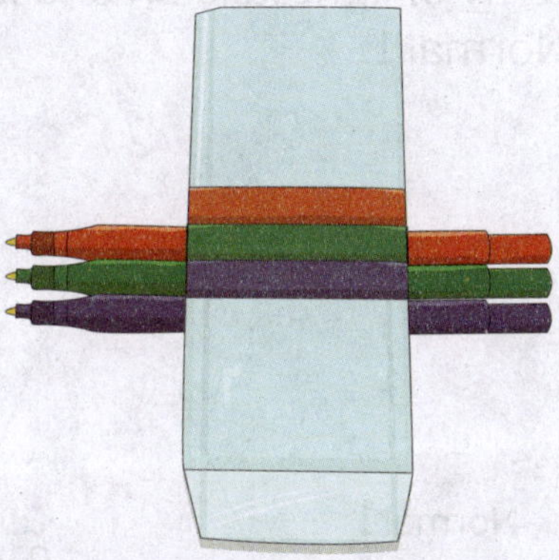

What Causes Lateral Shift?

We see objects through a glass slab when light rays from the object pass from air to glass and then from the glass to air to finally reach our eyes. The process is as follows:

1. The ray of light from the object enters the glass slab through point A.
2. Since glass is denser than air, the ray bends towards the normal N.
3. The ray passes through the glass and emerges out at point B.
4. Since air is rarer, the ray of light bends away from the normal N′.
5. The emergent ray is parallel to the original, incident ray.
6. The human eye can see only along the line of path of light that reaches the eyes. In this case, this line seems to come from a point shifted from the original point (Fig. 6.8).

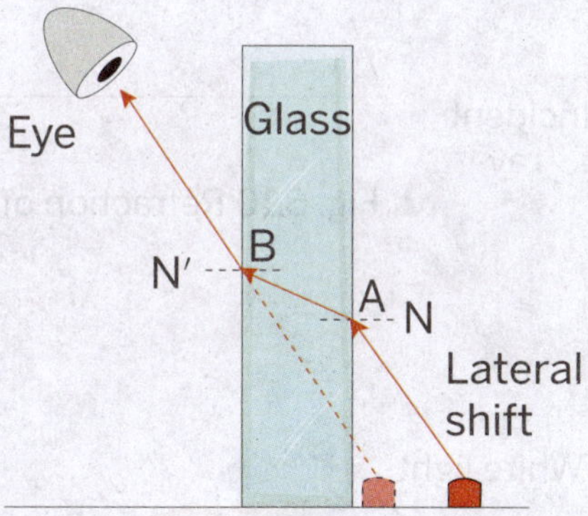

▲ Fig. 6.8 Lateral shift due to refraction

Summing up, we can say that lateral shift is caused because refraction takes place twice due to the change in the mediums.

Refraction Through a Prism

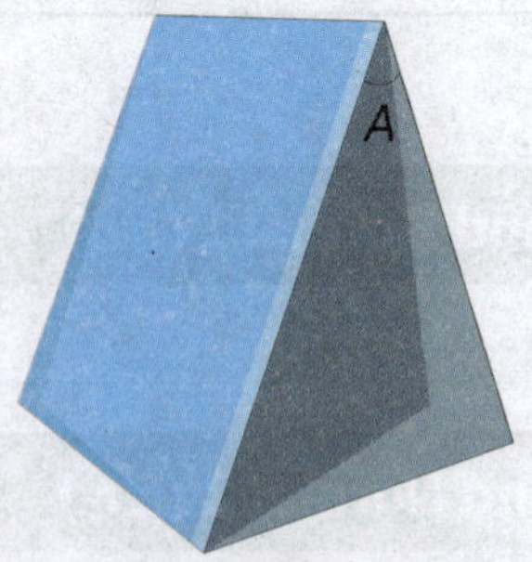

▲ Fig. 6.9 A triangular prism with an angle *A*

A prism is a transparent piece of glass or other material with plane surfaces. A normal triangular prism consists of two triangular surfaces, two rectangular faces and a rectangular base. The two rectangular faces are joined at an angle *A* called the **angle of the prism** (Fig. 6.9).

When a ray of light passes through a prism, it bends towards the normal as it enters the prism from one of the rectangular faces and away from the normal as it leaves the prism from the second rectangular face. Unlike a parallel-sided glass slab, the sides of the prism are at a certain angle to each other. So, in a prism, the direction of the emergent ray is different from that of the incident ray. A cross section of refraction in a prism is shown in Fig. 6.10. The process is as follows:

1. A ray of light falls on one face of the prism at an angle of incidence $\angle i$ with respect to Normal 1.

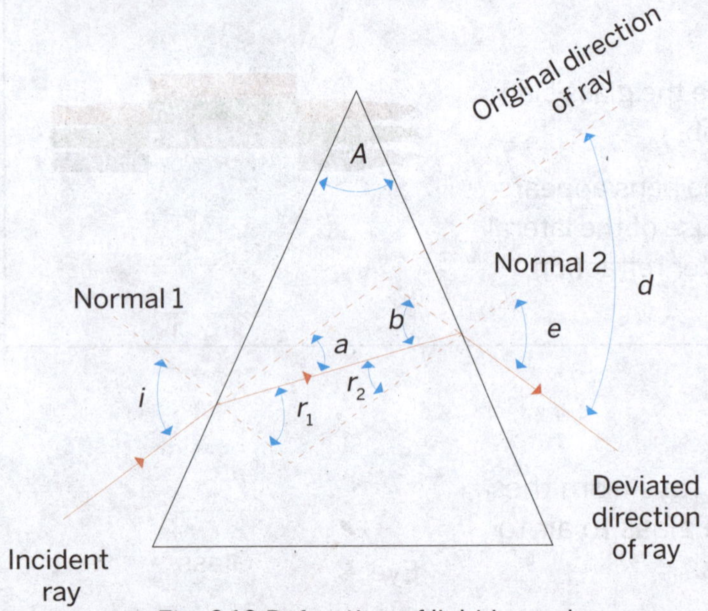

▲ Fig. 6.10 Refraction of light in a prism

2. The ray refracts with an angle of refraction $\angle r_1$ towards Normal 1 and passes through the prism.
3. It reaches the other face of the prism with an angle of incidence $\angle r_2$ with respect to Normal 2.
4. The ray refracts at an angle of refraction $\angle e$ away from Normal 2.
5. The emergent ray from the second face moves in a different direction, at an angle *d* with respect to the original direction of the incident ray. $\angle d$ is the **angle of deviation** of the emergent ray.
6. For refraction of light through a prism,
   $\angle i + \angle e = \angle A + \angle d$
   where, A is the angle of prism.

Dispersion of Light

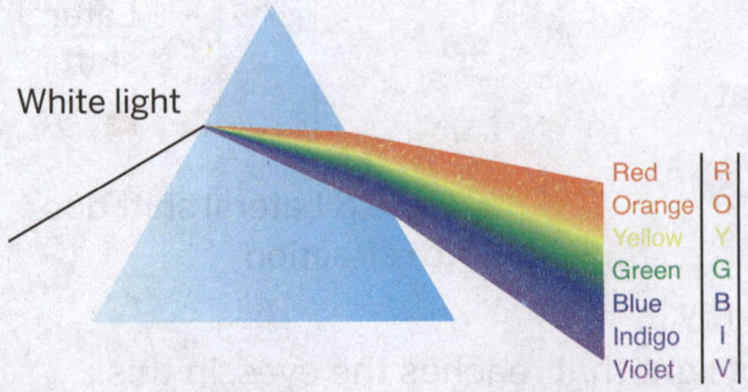

▲ Fig. 6.11 Dispersion of white light

When we expose a compact disc (CD) to sunlight, we see different colours on it. This is due to the fact that visible light is made up of different colours. The splitting of light into its component colours is called **dispersion of light**. When a beam of white light is passed through a prism, it splits into its seven component colours. If we project the light that passes through the prism on a white screen, we see a sequence of seven colours in the following order: violet, indigo, blue, green, yellow, orange and red. The range of colours obtained is called the **visible spectrum**.

Know the Scientist

It was **Sir Isaac Newton** (1643–1727) who showed that white light can be split into its constituent colours by passing it through a prism. He conducted an experiment in which he passed a narrow beam of sunlight through a prism and received the light coming out of the prism on a screen. He observed that the white beam of sunlight split into seven colours.

What Causes Dispersion?

The different colours of visible light have different wavelengths. For example, the light waves at the blue end of the visible spectrum are shorter and the light waves at the red end are longer (Fig. 6.12). Waves with different wavelengths move at different speeds in a prism. The speed of light waves in the blue region is lesser than the speed of light waves in the red region because of their shorter wavelengths. So, they travel slower in the prism and hence, bend more.

When visible light is incident on a prism face, violet light bends the most, followed by indigo, blue, green, yellow, orange and red. When light reaches the other face of the prism and emerges out of the prism, the violet light bends even further. So do the other colours from indigo to red. This results in the display of a full spectrum of light.

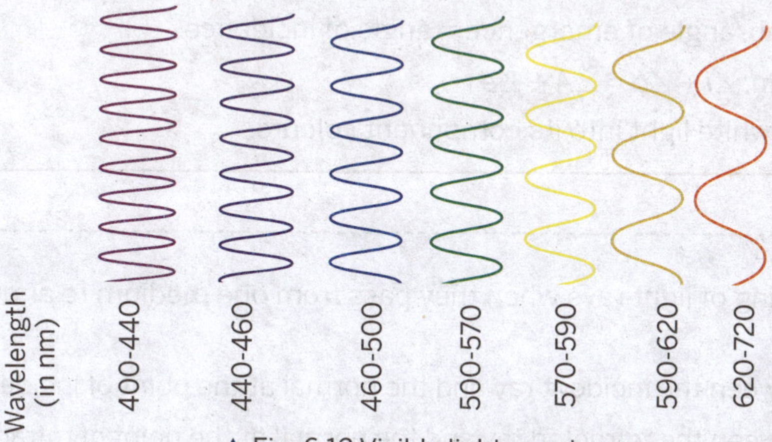

▲ Fig. 6.12 Visible light spectrum

Challenge Yourself

Dispersion is observed when light is passed through a prism. But no dispersion is observed when light is passed through a glass slab. Why?

Let us perform an activity to understand dispersion.

Activity 5

Aim: To understand dispersion through a prism

Materials required: Light source (a mercury lamp), cardboard with a narrow slit (opening), prism and screen

Procedure: Switch ON the light source and place the cardboard slit in front of it. Arrange the prism and the screen such that the light from the light source coming through the slit passes through the prism and then falls on the screen. Observe the pattern of the light on the screen.

Observation: When light is passed through a prism, the white light splits into its constituent colours and falls as a band of seven colours on the screen.

Conclusion: White light consists of seven colours.

▲ Fig. 6.13 Rainbow

Rainbow

The different colours in a rainbow are formed due to the dispersion of sunlight as it passes through small water droplets in the air after the rain stops. The droplets act as a prism and break light into its component colours. The different colours thus formed appear as bands across the sky, which we call a **rainbow**.

Revision Zone

Write T for True and F for False.

1. When light passes from air to glass, it bends away from the normal.
2. During refraction through a glass slab, angle of emergence = angle of incidence.
3. During the refraction through a prism, $\angle i + \angle d = \angle A + \angle e$
4. Dispersion of light is the splitting of white light into its component colours.

Keywords

Refraction: the phenomenon of bending of light rays when they pass from one medium to another having varying densities

Angle of incidence: angle formed between the incident ray and the normal at the point of incidence

Angle of refraction: angle formed between the refracted ray and the normal at the point of refraction

Refractive index: the ratio of the speed of light in vacuum to the speed of light in a medium

Dispersion: the process of splitting of white light into its component colours

Spectrum: the band of colours obtained on a white screen due to dispersion of light

In a Nutshell

- When light passes from a denser medium to a rarer medium, it bends away from the normal.
- When light passes from a rarer medium to a denser medium, it bends towards the normal.
- Light ray emerging from a glass slab after two refractions causes a lateral shift from the original direction of the ray.
- Rainbow is formed due to the dispersion of sunlight as it passes through small water droplets in the air after the rain stops.

Exercise

1 Choose the correct answer for each of the following.

a. When light passes from a rarer medium to a denser medium, it

i. bends away from the normal

ii. bends towards the normal

iii. always passes without deviation

iv. shifts laterally

b. The angle *r* formed between a refracted ray and a normal is the

i. angle of incidence

ii. angle of refraction

iii. normal angle

iv. None of these

c. The refractive index of water is

i. 1.0 ii. 1.5

iii. 1.3 iv. 1.6

d. In the spectrum of light, ________ has the shortest wavelength.

i. violet ii. yellow

iii. green iv. red

e. The phenomenon of splitting of white light is called

i. reflection ii. refraction

iii. dispersion

iv. rectilinear propagation of light

f. Rainbow is formed due to ________ of sunlight.

i. refraction ii. reflection

iii. dispersion iv. lateral shift

2 Fill in the blanks.

a. The phenomenon of bending of light when it passes from one optical medium to another is called ________ (reflection/refraction).

b. Light travels at ________ (different/same) speed(s) in different mediums.

c. The ratio of speed of light in vacuum to that in a medium is called ________ (refractive index/focal length).

d. The bend effect of a pencil in water is due to ________ (dispersion/refraction) of light.

e. The band of colours obtained by dispersion of light is called ________ (rainbow/spectrum).

3 Write T for True and F for False.

a. $\dfrac{\sin i}{\sin r} = \dfrac{v_1}{v_2}$

b. Light cannot be refracted by glass.

c. A rectangular glass slab can split white light into its seven component colours.

d. The speed of light in a denser medium is more than in a rarer medium.

e. The wavelength of green light is less than that of yellow light.

f. The speed of light waves in the blue region is more than that in the red region.

4 Define the following.

a. First law of refraction

b. Snell's law

c. Optical medium

d. Angle of incidence

e. Spectrum

5 Differentiate between the following.

a. Denser medium and rarer medium

b. Angle of incidence and angle of refraction

c. Refraction and dispersion

d. Refraction through a glass slab and through a prism

6 Name the following.

a. Angle between refracted ray and normal
b. This perpendicular distance between the emergent ray from a rectangular glass slab and the incident ray
c. The ratio of speed of light in vacuum to speed of light in a medium
d. Splitting of light into its component colours

7 Answer the following questions in brief.

a. What is point of incidence?
b. Give any two examples of the effects of refraction observed in nature.
c. What is lateral shift?
d. What is a normal in the refraction of a ray of light?
e. Define refractive index of a medium and give its formula.
f. What is dispersion?
g. Mention the order of colours in the spectrum of white light.

8 Answer the following questions in detail.

a. Draw ray diagrams to show the refraction of a light ray from
   i. a rarer to a denser medium and
   ii. a denser to a rarer medium.
b. What causes the bend effect in refraction?
c. What causes lateral shift? Explain it with the help of refraction of light through a glass slab?
d. Explain dispersion of light.
e. Describe an activity to obtain the spectrum of white light.
f. How are rainbows formed?

9 Think and answer.

White light passed through a prism will split into its component colours. Can we combine these colours to produce white light again?

10 In the Library

a. We know that light is a form of energy. There are different theories developed to explain the behaviour of light. Collect information about different theories of light and the scientists who proposed the theories.
b. Extend your knowledge by exploring the comparison between refraction of light and reflection of light.

11 Project

a. Observe the nature of refraction of light using two mediums: oil and water. Immerse a pencil and check the difference in refraction.
b. Create a rainbow in a glass

Materials required: Glass of water (filled up to ¾th), piece of mirror and torchlight

Procedure:

1. Place the glass of water on a table.
2. Keep the mirror in the glass as shown in the figure.
3. Switch off the light in the room and shine the torch on the mirror.
4. Move the torchlight around the glass until you see a rainbow formed on the mirror.

Worksheet

A **Subject Integration**

Mention the phenomenon of light in the given images.

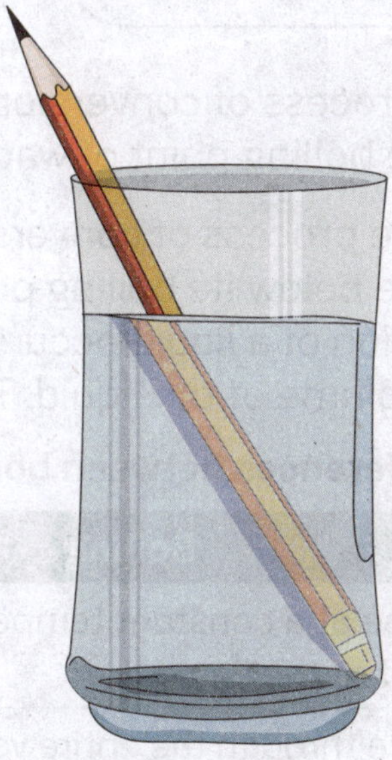

B **Life Skills**

Demonstrate an activity to show refraction of light.

Materials required: Water in a jar, scissors, cardboard, dark room, torch or flash light

Do this experiment in a dark room to achieve better results.

Why light travels slower in water than in air?

Heat Transfer

7

What I shall learn

- Difference between Boiling and Evaporation
- Thermal Expansion
- Types of Expansion
- Thermal Expansion of Solids, Liquids and Gases

Introduction

We have learned in the previous classes that the heat energy always flows from a region of higher temperature to a region of lower temperature, till both the regions attain the same temperature. This phenomenon is called **transfer of heat**. Heat can be transferred from one object to another by three modes: conduction, convection and radiation. In this chapter, we will learn more about heat energy and its effects.

Differences between Boiling and Evaporation

We have learned that if a liquid substance is continuously supplied heat energy, its temperature increases and at a particular temperature it starts converting into its gaseous state. The process of conversion of a liquid into its gaseous state at its boiling point is called **boiling**. The boiling point of water is 100 °C.

However, the process of conversion of a substance from its liquid state into gaseous state at a temperature below its boiling point is called **evaporation**. Evaporation is different from boiling as evaporation of a liquid occurs at the surface of the liquid, whereas boiling occurs through the entire volume of the liquid. Table 7.1 gives the differences between boiling and evaporation.

Table 7.1 Differences between boiling and evaporation

Boiling	Evaporation
It takes place at a constant temperature called the boiling point of the liquid.	It usually takes place below the boiling point of the liquid.
It takes place through the entire volume of the liquid.	It takes place only at the surface of the liquid.
It does not change the temperature of the liquid.	It cools down the liquid.
It takes place quickly.	It takes place slowly.

Thermal Expansion

We have already learned that matter exists in three states solid, liquid and gas. The molecular arrangement differs in all three states. In solids, the molecules are closely packed, in liquids the molecules are less closely packed than in solids and in gases the molecules are free to move around.

When a substance is heated, the molecules absorb heat energy and start vibrating faster. They move farther apart from each other leading to expansion of the substances. The solids expand less compared to liquids and liquids expand less compared to gases. This phenomenon of expansion of solids, liquids and gases upon heating is called **thermal expansion**.

Types of Expansion

Generally, materials expand on heating and contract on cooling. When a material is heated, it expands in terms of length, area or volume.

Linear expansion is the tendency of a material to expand lengthwise when heated.

Superficial expansion is the tendency of a material to expand its area when heated.

Volume expansion is the tendency of a material to expand its volume. It is also known as cubical expansion.

Let us perform simple activities to understand this.

Activity 1

Aim: To understand the linear expansion of materials (solid)

Materials required: Thin copper wire, a candle and a metre scale.

Procedure:

1. Measure the length of the copper wire.
2. Keep the copper wire above the flame of candle.
3. After few minutes measure the length of wire.

Observation: The length of the copper wire after heating is increased.

Conclusion: Linear expansion occurs when a material is heated.

Activity 2

Aim: To understand the superficial expansion of materials (solid)

Materials required: Bunsen burner, piece of paper, pair of tongs, coloured pens and thin metal sheet

Procedure:

1. Place the thin metal sheet on a paper and draw an outline on it.
2. Hold the metal sheet with the help of tongs above the Bunsen burner.
3. After a while, place the metal sheet on a paper and mark the outline with some other colour.
4. Check both the outlines to verify the size of the metal sheet.

Observation: The outline of the metal sheet after heating is slightly increased.

Conclusion: Superficial expansion occurs when a material is heated.

Thermal Expansion of Solids

Solids expand upon heating and contract upon cooling. Solids are held together by a strong intermolecular force. So, expansion in solids is not much and is sometimes not very prominent. Let us do a simple activity to understand expansion of solids upon heating.

Activity 3

Aim: To verify expansion of solids on heating

Materials required: Metal ball, metal ring and candle

Procedure:

First make sure that the metal ball can just pass through the ring, with a struggle. Now heat the metal ball for a while and try passing the ball through the ring. Allow the ball to cool down and try to pass it again through the ring.

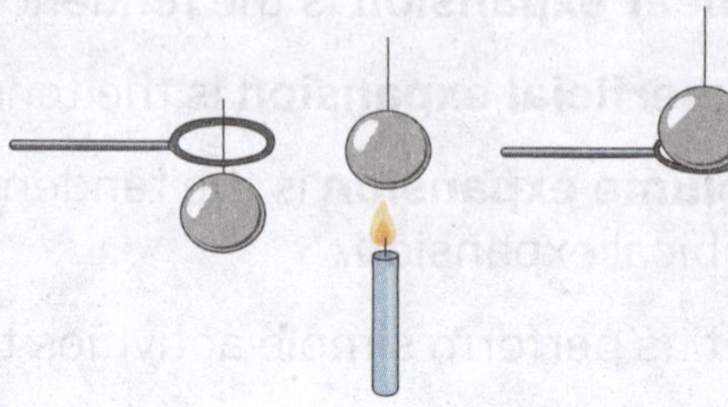

Observation: When the ball is heated, it does not pass through the ring. When the ball is cooled down, it passes though the ring.

Conclusion: Solids expand upon heating and contract upon cooling.

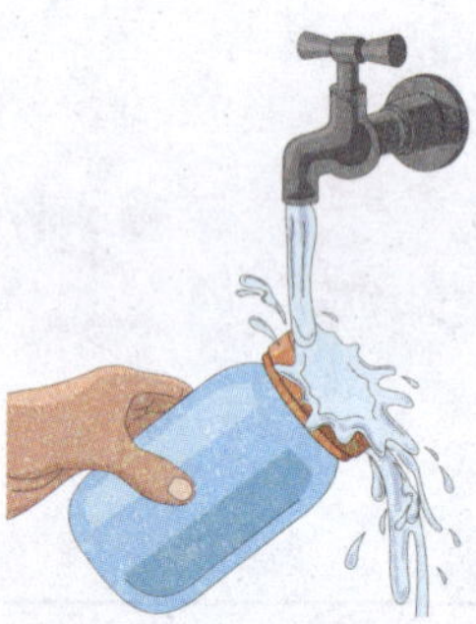

▲ Fig. 7.1 Running hot water over a bottle lid expands the lid

The rate of expansion differs from material to material. For example, expansion of brass will be more than that of iron at any temperature.

Some materials start expanding at low temperatures while some expand only at high temperatures.

Applications of Thermal Expansion in Solids

- **Thermal expansion in kitchens**: In a kitchen, it is sometimes seen that the lids of bottles get very tight and become difficult to open. To open the bottle, we run hot water over the lid, which enables it to expand and hence, it becomes easy for us to remove the lid (Fig. 7.1).

  Sometimes, we face the challenge of inserting the rubber tube in the gas stove. We usually heat the edge of the tube a little so that it expands and it becomes easy for us to insert the tube.

- **Power lines and telephone lines**: Power lines and telephone lines are usually connected between poles in a way that they hang a bit loose (Fig. 7.2). This is to prevent the wires from snapping as they contract during winter and expand during summer.

▲ Fig. 7.2 Power lines hung loose

- **Expansion joints on bridges**: Most of the large bridges have expansion joints (Fig. 7.3). In the absence of expansion joints, the bridge will have no space to expand during the day when it is hot. The expansion joints are like the teeth of two combs joined together.

  During the day, the bridge expands and the teeth of the expansion joints move towards each other and during night, the bridge cools and the teeth move away from each other. This acts as an inbuilt safety mechanism for the bridges.

▲ Fig. 7.3 Expansion joints on bridge

- **Railway tracks**: Railway tracks (Fig. 7.4) are laid in such a way that there is a gap between two track segments. This is to ensure that they do not bend while expanding during the day.

▲ Fig. 7.4 Gaps in railway track

Thermal Expansion of Liquids

In liquids, the molecules are held together by a weak intermolecular force. So, they can move around more freely than in solids. As a result, upon heating the volume of liquids increases more than that of solids at a given temperature.

Let us understand thermal expansion in liquids through a simple activity.

Activity 4

Aim: To verify if a given liquid expands on heating

Materials required: Conical flask, water, burner, tripod stand and marker

Procedure:

1. Fill the conical flask half with water.
2. Mark the level of water in the conical flask using the marker.
3. Now, place the conical flask on the tripod stand with the burner underneath.
4. Light the burner and start heating the conical flask on a low flame.
5. Compare the current level of water in the conical flask against the mark that indicates the initial level.

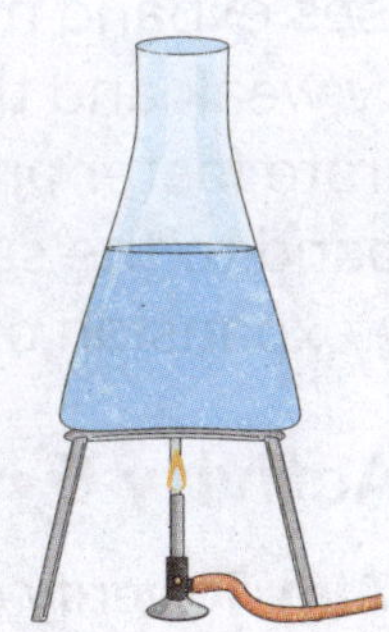

Observation: The level of water has slightly risen compared to the initial level.

Conclusion: Water expands upon heating.

The level of increase in volume differs from liquid to liquid. Let us understand this with a simple activity.

Activity 5

Aim: To verify the expansion of different liquids

Materials required: Three identical round-bottom flasks, water, alcohol, cooking oil and glass tub filled with water and a boiling setup

Procedure:

1. Fill one round-bottom flask each with water, alcohol and cooking oil.
2. Place the three flasks in the glass tub filled with water and start heating.
3. Compare the level of liquids in the flasks after some time.

Observation: The rise in the level of liquids varies for the three liquids.

Conclusion: Different liquids expand differently upon heating.

Applications of Thermal Expansion in Liquids

- **Thermometer**: A thermometer works on the principle of the thermal expansion of liquids. In a mercury thermometer, the mercury which is in the bulb of the thermometer, expands upon heating, rises through the capillary tube and gives us the reading. Similarly, alcohol expands in the alcohol thermometer.
- **Liquid in sealed bottles**: We buy bottled water and soft drinks. Have you ever noticed the level of the drinks in the bottles? The level of the liquid is usually below the neck of the bottle. This extra space is to adjust for the thermal expansion of the liquid in different conditions.
- **Boiling of water**: We do not boil water with the vessel filled to the brim. This is because water expands and can overflow.

Thermal Expansion of Gases

Gases expand more than solids and liquids. In gases, the intermolecular force of attraction is very weak and the molecules can move around freely. With the addition of heat, the molecules vibrate faster and move further apart. This increases the volume of the gases. All gases expand to the same level at a given temperature. Let us perform the following activity to verify the expansion of gases on heating.

Activity 6

Aim: To verify expansion of gases on heating

Materials required: Balloon, plastic bottle of 500 mℓ, bowl of warm water and bowl of ice

Procedure:

1. Take the plastic bottle of 500 mℓ. Fix the balloon on the mouth of the plastic bottle. Place the bottle inside a bowl of warm water. Observe the bottle and balloon after some time.
2. Take the bottle out and place it in the ice bowl. Allow it to cool. Observe the bottle and balloon.

Observation:

- When the bottle is placed in the bowl of warm water, the balloon inflates.
- When the bottle is removed from the warm water and cooled in the ice bowl, the balloon deflates.

Conclusion: The inflation and deflation of the balloon is because of the fact that air contained in the bottle expands upon heating and contracts upon cooling.

Applications of Thermal Expansion in Gases

- **Hot air balloon**: Hot air balloon has a burner at the bottom, which upon being lighted starts heating up the air inside the balloon. Upon heating, the air inside the balloon expands and becomes lighter. So, it rises up pulling the balloon upwards and making it float.
- **Chinese lantern**: Chinese lantern works in the same way as the hot air balloon. The fire underneath heats up the air inside the lantern, which expands, moves upwards and enables the lantern to float.

▲ Fig. 7.5 Hot gas balloon

Revision Zone

Write T for True and F for False.

1. The process by which a solid gets converted to a liquid upon heating is called melting.
2. Evaporation is a process in which a substance gets converted from solid state to gaseous state.
3. Upon heating, solids expand more than liquids and gases.
4. Hot air balloons work on the principle of thermal expansion of gases.

Keywords

Boiling: process of conversion of a liquid into gaseous state at its boiling point.

Evaporation: process of conversion of a liquid to its gaseous state at a temperature below the boiling point.

Thermal Expansion: the phenomenon of expansion of solids, liquids and gases upon heating

In a Nutshell

- Linear expansion is the tendency of a material to expand its length.
- Superficial expansion is the tendency of a material to expand its area.
- Volume expansion is the tendency of a material to expand its volume.
- Solids expand upon heating and contract upon cooling.

Exercise

1 Choose the correct answer for each of the following.

a. The increase in size of matter on heating is termed as ________ .

i. Thermal expansion

ii. Thermal work

iii. Thermal contraction

iv. Thermal Energy

b. Volume expansion is also known as ________ .

i. Thermal expansion

ii. Linear Expansion

iii. Cubical expansion

iv. Superficial expansion

c. In solids, transfer of heat takes place by

i. conduction ii. radiation

iii. convection iv. All the above

d. Superficial expansion is the expansion of matter in its ________

i. length ii. volume

iii. area iv. capacity

e. The lid of a bottle got tightened. Which of the following methods will help in opening the bottle?

i. Heat the bottle from the bottom

ii. Place the bottle in a bowl containing ice cubes

iii. Show the lid part to running hot water

iv. Show the lid part to running cold water

2 Fill in the blanks.

a. Thermal expansion is maximum in ________ . (gases/liquids)

b. Most of the ________ material expand when heated. (solid/liquid)

c. A thermometer works on the principle of the thermal expansion of ________ . (liquids/gases)

d. Thermal expansion of ________ (solids/gases) takes place in Chinese Lantern.

e. The area of the solid material ________ on heating. (expands/contracts)

f. Dark colours are good ________ (reflectors/absorbers) of heat.

g. In liquids, the molecules are held together by a ________ (weaker/ stronger) intermolecular force.

h. The air inside the hot air balloon ________ (contracts/expands) upon heating.

3 Write T for True and F for False.

a. Solids expand more than liquids and gases.

b. In gases, the molecules are tightly packed.

c. Power lines are hung loose between poles to prevent it from snapping during summer.

d. Movement of mercury in a thermometer upon heating is an example of thermal expansion of liquids.

e. Expansion of all liquids and gases are different.

f. Volume of a solid cannot be increased on heating.

4 Match the following.

a.	Expansion in overhead cables	i.	linear expansion
b.	Chinese Lantern	ii.	Cubical expansion
c.	Thermometer	iii.	Thermal expansion and when heated
d.	Metallic ball	iv.	Thermal expansion of liquids

5 Define the following.

a. Thermal Expansion
b. Linear Expansion
c. Superficial Expansion
d. Volume Expansion

6 Give reason for the following.

a. Why do soft drink bottles burst in summer?
b. Why does a liquid or a gas show cubical expansion only?
c. Why do gases expand more than liquids or solids?
d. Why are tiny gaps left in between rails on a railway line?

7 Name the following.

a. The liquid used in thermometer.
b. The tendency of a material to expand its length.
c. The tendency of a material to expand its area.
d. The tendency of a material to expand its volume.
e. The state of matter that expands the least on heating.

8 Answer the following questions in brief.

a. What is superficial expansion?
b. Write any two applications of thermal expansion of liquids.
c. What is thermal expansion?
d. Give two real-life applications of thermal expansion of solids.

9 Answer the following questions in detail.

a. List any four applications of thermal expansion in day-to-day life.
b. What are the differences between boiling and evaporation?
c. With a neat diagram, describe an experiment to prove that the solids expand on heating.
d. Write an activity to show the linear expansion of a material.
e. Write an activity to show the superficial expansion of a solid material.

10 Think and answer.

When hot water is poured in a thick glass tumbler, it cracks.

(Hint: Think about Thermal expansion.)

11 Project

Make an electric circuit that closes on heating and opens on cooling. Use a brass strip as connector in the circuit.

Take a wooden base. Fix a battery holder with a battery. Connect a wire from one end of the battery holder to a bulb holder. Connect the brass strip to a wire such that the other end of the wire is connected to the bulb holder. The other end of the brass strip should be left very close to the end of the battery but should not touch it. Upon heating, the brass strip expands and closes the circuit. Similarly, upon cooling, it breaks the circuit.

Worksheet

A Subject Integration

1. Give reason for the following question.

   Why cold drink bottles are not filled to the brim?

2. Write real-life applications of thermal expansion of liquids and gases in the space provided below.

B Life Skills

Make a role play to understand expansion of solids. Ask a student to play the role of a bangle seller. Let a girl student to be a customer. Ask her to get some broken bangles to the seller for fixing. How will the seller fix the broken bangles?

Materials Required: Glass bangles, candle

[Hint: Linear expansion of solids]

Sound

8

What I shall learn

- Pitch and Frequency of sound
- Quality or timbre of sound
- Loudness and Amplitude
- Noise pollution and its harmful effects

Introduction

Every day we hear a variety of sounds while we go about our daily routine. Different objects produce different types of sound. Some sounds are pleasant and some are unpleasant. The frequency, pitch and intensity level of sound determines whether the sound is pleasant or not.

In this chapter, we will learn about the frequency, pitch and intensity level of sound.

Pitch and Frequency

We have learned that **frequency** is the number of vibrations made by a vibrating object in one second. A low frequency wave has less number of vibrations per second and high frequency wave has more number of vibrations per second. Frequency varies for each sound and the unit of frequency is **hertz (Hz)**.

The shrillness of sound experienced by the listener is called the **pitch** of the sound. As the frequency of sound increases, its pitch also increases. A sound with low frequency will have a low pitch, such as water dripping from a pipe. A sound with high frequency will have a high pitch, such as a crying baby. With increase in pitch, the shrillness increases. The frequency of a female voice usually is more than the frequency of a male voice. Hence, it is shriller than the male voice.

Know the Scientist

Heinrich Rudolf Hertz (1857–1894), a German physicist, produced electromagnetic waves in the laboratory. He proved that electricity and heat are electromagnetic radiations. Thus, Hertz immensely contributed towards the development of radio and television. Hertz measured the velocity of electromagnetic radiation and found it to be the same as the velocity of light.

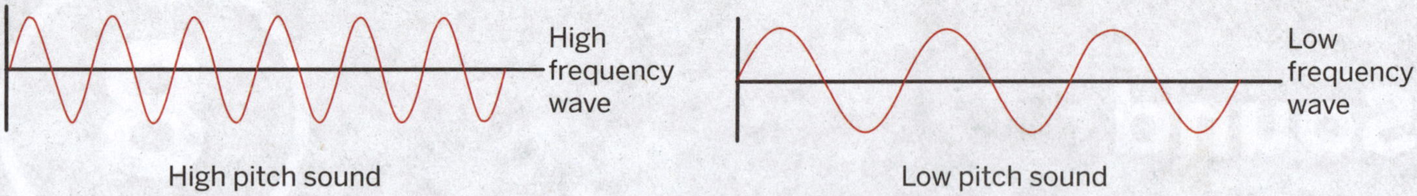

▲ Fig. 8.1 High pitch and low pitch sound waves

▲ Fig. 8.2 Musical instruments

Musical Instruments

Musical instruments can be classified into three categories based on how the sound is produced by them. An instrument like guitar and violin produces sound by the vibration of the stretched strings. Such instruments are called **string instruments**. An instrument like flute and trumpet produces sound by the vibration of air column inside them. Such instruments are called **wind instruments**. An instrument like drums and tabla produces sound by the vibration of stretched membrane. Such instruments are termed as **percussion instruments**.

Pitch and frequency in relation to working of instruments

In musical instruments like guitar and violin, we can see strings of different thicknesses. The thinner strings on the instruments can produce shriller sounds than the thicker strings. If the string is stretched more, it vibrates with more frequency and produces high-pitched sound. In guitar, when the lengths of the strings are shortened by tightening the screw knob, the frequency becomes high. As the frequency increases, its pitch also increases. When the lengths are increased by loosening the screw knob, the frequency becomes less and hence the pitch also decreases. Musicians tune musical instruments by adjusting the tension of the strings of guitar, violin, etc. and tension of the skin of tabla, drum, etc. By tuning these instruments, they ensure that the instruments produce sounds with desirable pitch. Pitch is important when people sing together in a choir.

Quality or Timbre of Sound

Quality or timbre of sounds helps us to distinguish between two sounds having the same pitch and loudness. For example, sounds of the same pitch and loudness are produced from a piano and a guitar. Even if we are not allowed to see the instruments, we would still be able to distinguish between the sounds of the guitar and the

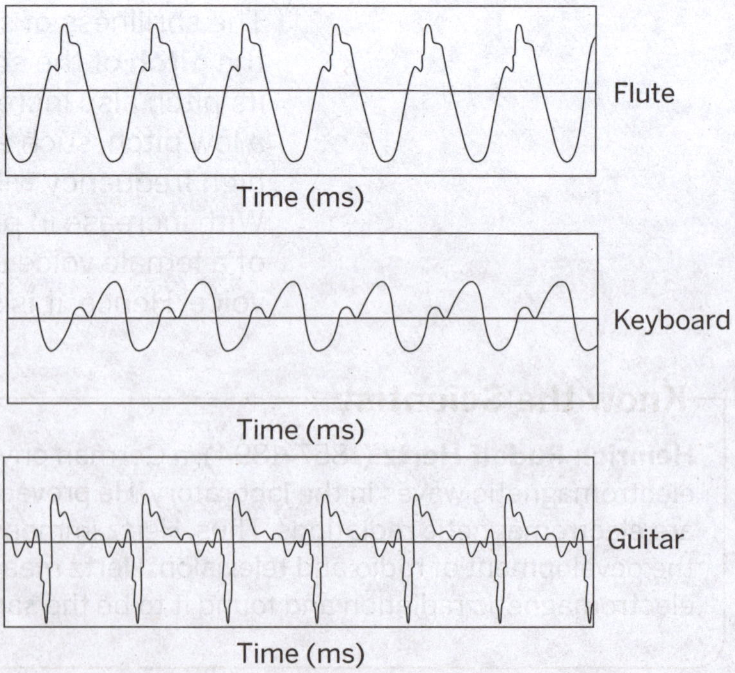

▲ Fig. 8.3 Timbre of three different musical instruments

piano. This is due to the difference in the timbre or quality of the sounds produced by a guitar and a piano.

Fig. 8.3 shows the timbre or quality of sounds produced by three different musical instruments that have the same amplitude and frequency.

Activity 1

Aim: To make a musical drum

Materials required: Cylindrical aluminium cans, thick balloons, rubber band, crumbled tissue papers, pencil and insulation tape

Procedure:

1. Use the balloon as a membrane over the aluminium can. Stretch a balloon and lay it flat on one side of the aluminium can. Wrap a rubber band around the balloon to keep the balloon and can intact. Cover the other cans with balloons but vary the stretch each time.
2. Make a pair of drumsticks by wrapping the crumpled tissue papers at the end of the pencil. Beat the membranes on the cans with these drumsticks.
3. If possible, take different set of cans and cover the cans with other materials like plastic and artificial leather.

Observation and conclusion: The quality and loudness of the sound from the drum depends on various factors like nature of material used and the stretch of the membranes.

Mono tone

Tone is determined with respect to the pitch, quality and strength of the sound. **Mono tone** sounds are the sounds that are produced in an unvaried manner. That is, if the pitch, quality and strength of the sound remain unchanged, then the sound is known as mono tone sound.

In other words, mono tone is the one which does not have any variation in the pitch or loudness. Suppose in a seminar hall, if a person gives speech with variation in pitch, the presentation would be effective and interesting. However, if the presenter uses mono tone sound in his speech, the presentation will be boring. Thus, the orator varies his loudness to grab the attention of the audience while delivering speech.

Loudness and Amplitude

The ear perceives loudness, and helps to identify low intensity and high intensity sounds. Amplitude determines the loudness of a sound. As amplitude increases, the loudness of the sound also increases. Loudness of a sound is directly proportional to the square of its amplitude. If the amplitude is doubled, then the loudness increases by a factor of 4.

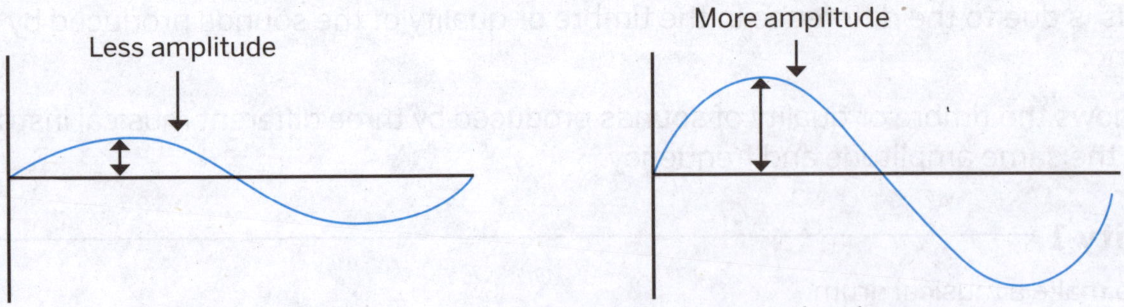

▲ Fig. 8.4 Loudness of a sound depends on its amplitude

Activity 2

Aim: To show that loudness of sound depends on the amplitude of sound

Materials required: A guitar or a violin

Procedure: Pluck the string of a guitar or violin softly. Observe the sound produced by the string. Now, pluck the same string hard. Observe the sound produced.

Observations: The sound produced when the string is plucked softly is soft sound and the sound produced when the string is plucked hard is loud.

Conclusion: Loudness of sound increases with the increase in amplitude of vibration.

Music and Noise

Do we find all sounds that we hear pleasant to our ears? Some sounds are pleasant to hear, while others are unpleasant. Sound that gives a pleasant feeling is usually called **musical sound** and sound that gives an unpleasant feeling is called **noise**. Table 8.1 gives the differences between music and noise.

Table 8.1 Differences between music and noise

Music	Noise
Musical sound is periodic.	Noise is non-periodic.
Amplitude is regular and rhythmic.	Amplitude is abrupt and irregular.
Pleasing to ears.	Unpleasing to ears.
Example: Sounds produced by musical instruments	Examples: Sounds from factories and vehicles

Noise Pollution

We know that noise is an unwanted, unpleasant, irritating and loud sound. Too much noise is harmful for ears and leads to noise pollution. Some of the major sources of noise pollution are sounds produced by running vehicles and their horns, various devices like vacuum cleaners, drilling machines, mixers and grinders, and machines used in industries.

Our ears cannot tolerate very loud sounds. The intensity or the level of sound is expressed in **decibel** (dB). Any sound higher than 120 dB is very loud and can cause pain in the ears. Table 8.2 gives the sounds produced by various sources and their levels.

Table 8.2 Sources of sound and their sound levels

Source	Sound level (dB)
Jet aircraft	140
Passing truck	100
Alarm clock	80
Vacuum cleaner	70
Conversational speech	60
Whisper	20

Watch Out!

- Do not expose yourself to very loud sound such as intense music for a long time.
- Always listen to music at a moderate volume.
- Avoid keeping sources of sound such as earphones and mobile phones close to the ears for a long time.

Prolonged exposure to a noise-polluted environment may lead to serious health problems. Some of these are given below.

- Long exposure to noise can reduce our concentration and can cause restlessness. It can also cause frequent headaches, hearing problems, etc.
- Exposure to high noise level may lead to sleep disturbance and discomfort.
- Sudden exposure to very high noise levels may lead to temporary or even permanent hearing disability.
- Prolonged exposure to a noisy environment leads to hypertension, high stress levels, and behavioural and emotional problems.
- Noise pollution leads to increased heartbeat, constriction of blood vessels, dilation of pupils, etc.

How to Reduce Noise Pollution

If the noise level in our environment is not controlled, it may damage our health. We can take some steps to reduce the noise level around us.

- Try to avoid very loud music.
- Planting more trees helps to reduce noise as they absorb sound.
- Minimize the use of defective machines and engines that produce more unwanted sound.
- Avoid unnecessary honking while driving.
- Wear ear plugs to protect the ears when working in a noisy surrounding.

Revision Zone

Fill in the blanks.

1. Loudness of a sound depends on its ________________ (amplitude/frequency).
2. Pitch of a sound is directly proportional to ________________ (amplitude/frequency).
3. The SI unit of ________________ (frequency/amplitude) is hertz.
4. The intensity level of sound is measured in ________________. (hertz/decibels)

Keywords

Sound: form of energy that produces a sensation of hearing to our ears

Frequency: number of vibrations completed by a vibrating particle in one second

Pitch: shrillness of sound experienced by the listener

Amplitude: the maximum displacement of a vibrating particle from its mean position to one of the extreme positions

decibel: unit of intensity level of sound

In a Nutshell

- Sound is produced by the vibration of particles present in objects.
- Frequency is measured in hertz.
- Pitch and frequency are directly proportional to each other.
- Loudness of sound increases with the increase in the amplitude.
- Loudness of sound is determined by its amplitude and pitch by its frequency.
- Timbre of sound helps us to distinguish between two sounds that have the same pitch and loudness.

Exercise

1 Choose the correct answer for each of the following.

a. Pitch increases with the

i. increase in frequency

ii. decrease in frequency

iii. constant frequency

iv. none of the above

b. Pitch and frequency are

i. directly proportional

ii. inversely proportional

iii. constant

iv. not related to each other

c. The level of sound is expressed in

i. hertz ii. metre/second

iii. decibel iv. newton

d. Number of vibrations completed by a particle in one second is known as

i. Amplitude ii. Pitch

iii. Frequency iv. Intensity

e. Intensity level of sound is measured in

i. m ii. s

iii. Hz iv. dB

2 Write T for True and F for False.

a. Lower is the frequency of vibration, higher is the pitch.

b. The unit of frequency is decibel.

c. Monotone sound has varied pitches.

d. Loudness of sound is determined by its amplitude.

e. Sounds with the same pitch and loudness always have the same timbre.

3 Match the following.

a. Intensity of sound	i. Frequency
b. Unit of frequency	ii. decibel
c. Pitch	iii. Amplitude
d. Loudness	iv. hertz

4 Define the following.

a. Decibel

b. Frequency

c. Amplitude

d. Mono tone

e. Pitch

5 Answer the following questions in brief.

a. What do you mean by quality of sound wave?

b. How does pitch of a sound vary with frequency?

c. How does loudness of a sound vary with amplitude?

d. How can you distinguish between the sounds of piano and guitar having the same pitch and loudness?

e. Differentiate between music and noise.

f. Mention any two harmful effects of noise pollution.

6 Answer the following questions in detail.

a. Tabulate different sounds with their intensity level.

b. Write a note on mono tone.

c. How pitch and frequency are related to the musical instruments?

d. Write an activity to show the construction of a drum.

e. Show that loudness of sound depends on the amplitude of the sound.

f. What is noise pollution? Explain the necessary measures that must be taken to reduce it.

7 Think and answer.

a. Suppose two objects are colliding in space just above Earth's atmosphere. Can we hear the sound produced due to the collision? Justify.

(Hint: Sound needs medium for propagation.)

b. Why do some people put their ear on to the track to hear a train approaching from a far-off distance?

(Hint: Speed of sound varies according to the medium.)

8 Project

Make a water bottle *jaltarang*.

When a glass bottle is tapped with a spoon, a sound of a particular pitch is produced. Follow these steps to make your own *jaltarang*.

Materials required: 6 glass bottles, water, spoon and marker

Fill the water bottles with decreasing levels of water as shown in the figure, starting from the maximum level.

Take the spoon and gently strike the bottles one after the other.

The lesser the water in the bottle, the higher will be the pitch.

Make your own music on your *jaltarang* and play along!

9 In the Library

People who construct halls for performance of arts and music study the acoustics of the halls. Collect details about acoustics (study of sound).

Worksheet

A Subject Integration

How will you change the pitch of tabla and guitar? Which part of the following musical instruments is used to change their pitch? Mark the same in the given images also.

B Life Skills

Try to compose a music using the given materials.

Materials Required:

- Glass of water
- Soda lids
- Empty water bottle
- Stick
- Rubber band or thread

More about Electricity

9

What I shall learn

- Electricity at Home
- Static Electricity
- Charging of objects
- Electroscope
- Lightning
- Battery and its uses
- Safety Measures while handling Electricity

Introduction

Electrical energy plays a very important role in our everyday life. Most of the appliances we use requires electrical energy to work. For example, all appliances like television, computer, refrigerator, micro-oven, fan, Air conditioner, and electrical iron require electrical energy. We receive the electricity from power station. However, we often use electrical appliances without considering the electric cost of such running devices. Using energy wisely not only reduces the electric bill but also helps in conserving energy. In this chapter, we will learn more about the household consumption of electric energy and to calculate energy consumption using household electricity bill.

Electricity at Home

Electricity that we use at home is generated at power stations like hydroelectric power stations, thermal power stations and nuclear power plants. Usually these power stations are far away from our houses and the places where electricity is used. The electricity produced at these power stations is carried using cables and supplied for different purposes like domestic purpose and industrial purpose.

AC Mains

The electricity that we use at home is called **alternating current** (AC) received at the AC mains. This electricity is generated at power stations and supplied to houses using cables. From the AC mains, it is distributed to different parts of our house through wires. Mains electricity has a standard voltage of 220 V and a frequency of 50 Hz. These values differ in different countries.

Domestic Circuit

Three wires are used in household electric wiring—live (phase), neutral and earth wires. These three wires are different in colour in order to identify them easily. Generally, red or brown colour is used for the live wire, black or blue for neutral wire and green or yellow for the earth wire. The devices that we use are connected between the live (phase) and the neutral wires. The earth wire, which is used for safety, is thicker than the live and the neutral wires, and is made of copper. It is connected to a thick copper rod or a copper plate buried deep under the earth.

A parallel circuit connection is used in domestic circuits. Fig. 9.1 gives a schematic diagram of a domestic circuit.

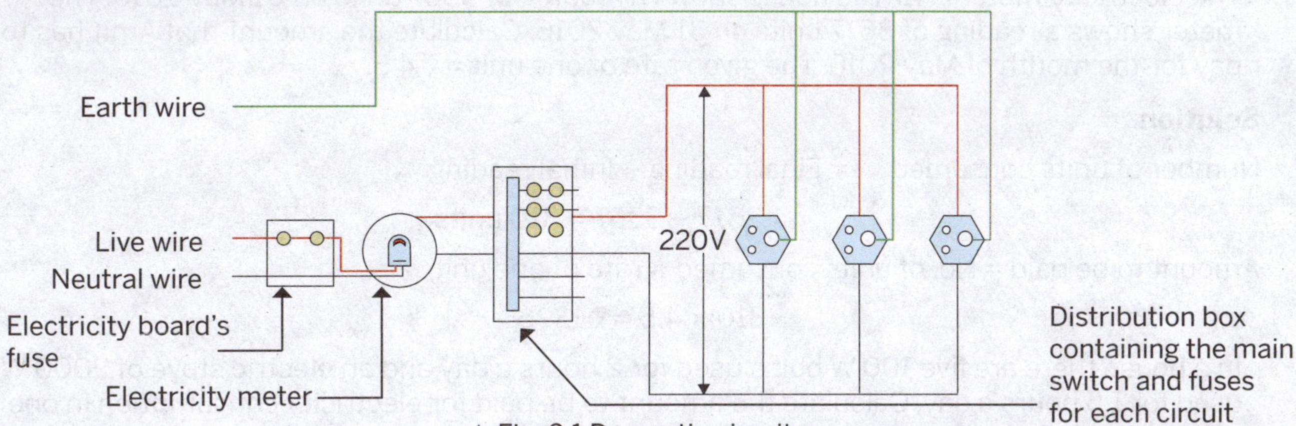

▲ Fig. 9.1 Domestic circuit

Electric Power

Electrical energy consumed per unit time is called the electric power. The SI unit of electric power is **watt (W)**. One watt is equal to one joule per second. That is, a device having a power of 100 W consumes 100 joules of electrical energy in one second.

Electrical energy consumed in our homes is expressed in a unit called **kilowatt-hour (kWh)**. One kilowatt-hour is the electrical energy consumed by a device of power 1000 W when operated for one hour. We have,

1 W = 1 J/s or 1 Ws = 1 J

So,

1 kWh = 36,00,000 J

Electricity Meter

Domestic and industrial consumption of electrical energy is measured using the energy meters or electricity meters installed at the places that use electricity. It gives the number of units of electrical energy or kWh of electrical energy consumed in a period of time, say one month (billing period). The number of units consumed multiplied by the rate of one unit gives the amount to be paid to the electricity board authority.

▲ Fig. 9.2 Electricity meter

Solved Problems

1. Raj uses five 100 W bulbs in his house for two hours per day. What is the electrical energy consumed in a day and in one month?

Solution:

Total power used by all the five bulbs = 5 × 100 = 500 W

Electrical energy used = Electric power × time

Electrical energy used in one day = 500 × 2 = 1000 Wh = 1 kWh

Electrical energy used in one month = 1 × 30 = 30 kWh

2. The electricity meter in Amit's house shows a reading of 3367 units on 01 May 2016. The meter shows a reading of 3677 units on 31 May 2016. Calculate the amount that Amit has to pay for the month of May 2016. The given rate of one unit = ₹ 4.5.

Solution:

Number of units consumed = Final reading – Initial reading

= 3677 – 3367 = 310 units

Amount to be paid = No. of units consumed × rate of one unit

= 310 × 4.5 = ₹ 1395

3. In a house there are five 100 W bulbs used for 2 hours a day and an electric stove of 2000 W used for 1.5 hours a day. Calculate the amount to be paid for electricity consumption in one month. The price of one unit of electricity = ₹ 4.5.

Solution:

Total energy used in one day = Energy used by bulbs + Energy used by stove

Energy used by five bulbs = 5 × 100 W × 2 h = 1000 Wh = 1 kWh

Energy used by the stove = 2000 W × 1.5 h = 3000 Wh = 3 kWh

So, total energy consumed in a day = 1 kWh + 3 kWh = 4 kWh

Energy consumed in one month = 4 × 30 = 120 kWh = 120 units

Amount to be paid = 120 × 4.5 = ₹ 540

Electric Fuse

What happens to a small torch bulb if we connect it across more number of cells? The filament of the bulb gets damaged due to the excess amount of current flowing through it. Such a bulb is usually called a fused bulb. The filament of a fused bulb is broken or burned due to the excess flow of current. The current in excess amount can cause damage to the electrical appliances and the household electrical circuits. A **fuse** or an **electric fuse** is a safety device, which is connected in the circuit, to protect the electrical circuit and the devices in the circuit from excess current passing through it.

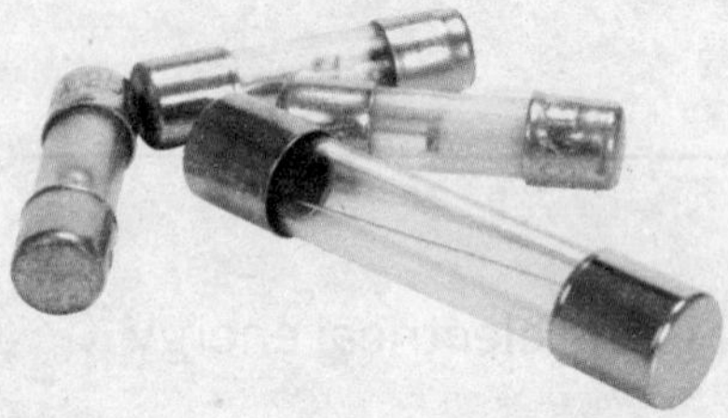

▲ Fig. 9.3 Electric fuse

Electric fuse works on the principle of the heating effect of electric current. The quantity of heat produced in a conductor by a current depends on the amount of current flowing through the conductor. A fuse consists of a narrow wire called the fuse wire which gets heated and breaks off if any excess current flows through the circuit. When it is broken, the circuit becomes a broken or open circuit and no current flows through it and the devices in the circuit remain safe. The fuse wire is designed for only a particular amount of current to flow through. If more current flows through it than the desired current, more heat is produced in the wire and it breaks thereby preventing the devices from damage which may occur due to excessive flow of current.

Miniature Circuit Breakers

Miniature circuit breaker (MCB) is a device that automatically cuts off the current in the circuit if excess current flows through the circuit. It can be reset easily unlike a fuse.

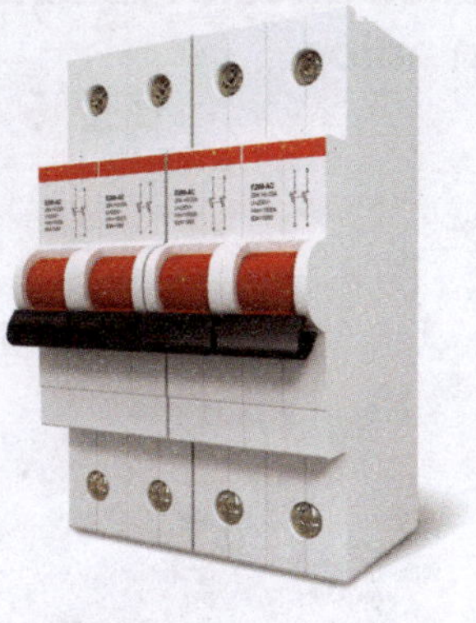

▲ Fig. 9.4 MCB

Three pin plug with live, neutral and earth wires

A lot of appliances need three wires to work safely. Only two of the wires are used when the appliance works. These are the live (brown) and the neutral (blue) wires.

The live wire carries current to the appliance at a high voltage.

The neutral wire completes the circuit and carries current away from the appliance.

The third wire, called the earth wire (green/yellow) is a safety wire and connects the metal case of the appliance to the earth. This prevents chance of an electric shock in case of any damage or any other short circuit inside the device.

▲ Fig. 9.5 Inside of a three pin plug

Static Electricity

During dry days, we often experience small shocks when we touch metallic door knobs or metallic water taps. There is no electric current flowing through the door knob or water tap. Then, how do we get those shocks? The reason behind this is that electric charges build up on door knobs and taps. When we touch door knobs and taps, these charges pass on to our body and we feel a shock. These built up charges are called **static charges** since they are stationary on the object. This imbalance of charges in a body because of the accumulation of charges in the body is called **static electricity**.

Nature of Charges

Matter is made up of particles called atoms that are composed of subatomic particles called protons, neutrons and electrons. Protons are positively-charged particles and electrons are negatively-charged particles. Neutrons are neutral particles or particles with no charge.

Protons and neutrons together form a massive centre or core of the atom called the **nucleus** and the electrons, which are lighter particles, move around the nucleus in orbits. The electrons in the orbits close to the nucleus of an atom are bound very strongly to the nucleus and are called **bound electrons**. The electrons in the outer orbit of atoms of some substances can acquire enough energy to free themselves from the atoms. These electrons are called **free electrons**.

Normally, in an atom, the number of protons (positive charges) and the number of electrons (negative charges) is same so that the atom is electrically neutral. If the number of electrons is more or less than the number of protons, then the atom is charged. A charged atom is called an **ion**. A positively charged ion is called a **cation** and a negatively charged ion is called an **anion**.

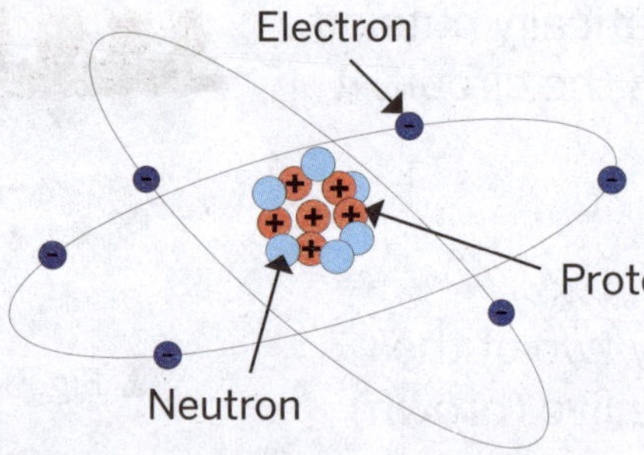

▲ Fig. 9.6 Structure of an atom

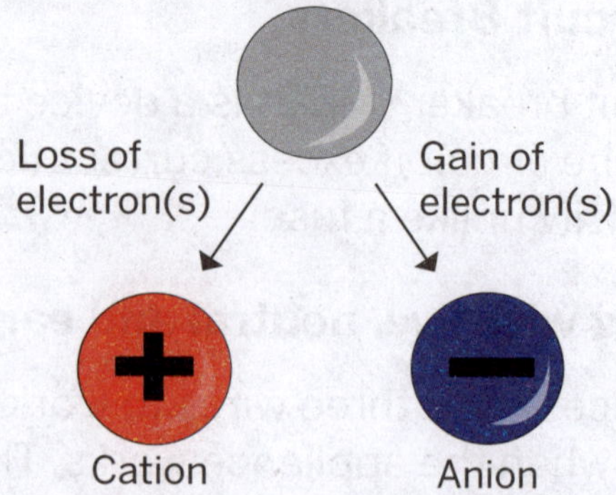

▲ Fig. 9.7 Formation of cations and anions

Activity 1

Aim: To show the presence of static charge on a plastic scale rubbed with hair

Materials required: Plastic scale and bits of paper

Procedure:

1. Rub the scale on your hair.
2. Bring the scale near the bits of paper.

Observation: The bits of paper stick to the scale.

Conclusion: Upon rubbing the scale on hair, it becomes electrically charged. The charges acquired by the scale are called static charges because they are stationary.

Electric charges exhibit the property of attraction and repulsion when they are brought close to each other. Electric charges attract or repel each other according to the nature of the charges. Let us understand this through the following activity.

Activity 2

Aim: To show that like charges repel and unlike charges attract

Materials required: Two ebonite rods, two glass rods, wool, silk and thread

Procedure:

1. Rub one ebonite rod with wool and hang it with a thread. Rub the other ebonite rod with wool and bring it near the hung rod [Fig. (a)]. Observe how the rods interact. (Note: The ebonite rod rubbed with wool acquires a negative charge due to friction.)
2. Rub one glass rod with silk and hang it with a thread. Rub the other glass rod with silk and bring it near the hung glass rod. Observe how the rods interact. (Note: The glass rod rubbed with silk acquires a positive charge due to friction.)
3. Now, hang an ebonite rod rubbed with wool and bring a glass rod rubbed with silk closer to it [Fig. (b)]. Observe how the rods interact.

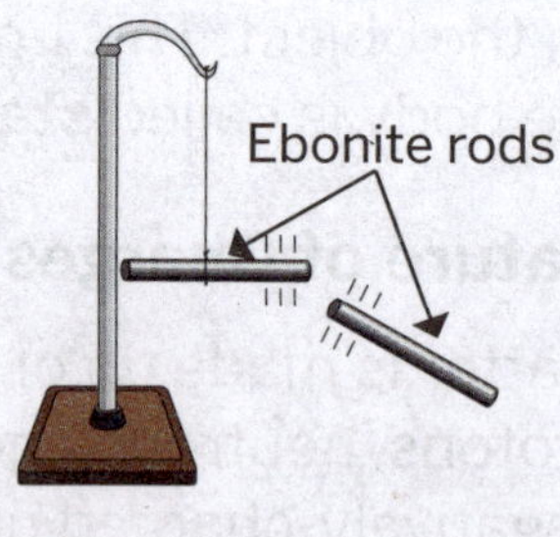

(a)

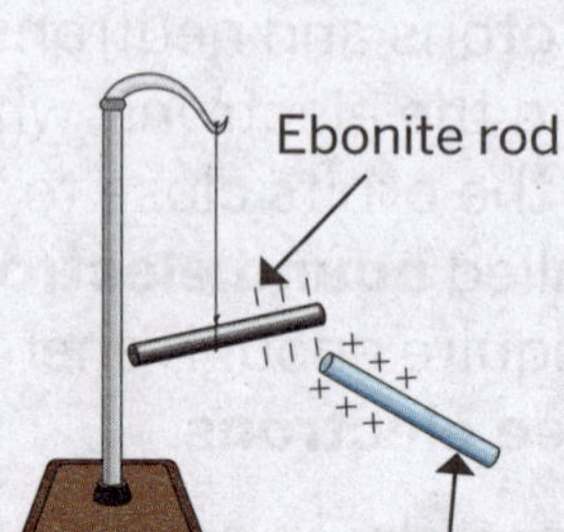

(b)

Observation:

Scenario	Attraction/Repulsion
Ebonite rod rubbed with wool brought close to another ebonite rod rubbed with wool	
Glass rod rubbed with silk brought close to another glass rod rubbed with silk	
Ebonite rod rubbed with wool brought close to glass rod rubbed with silk	

Conclusion: Like charges repel and unlike charges attract.

In Activity 2, the ebonite rods acquired negative charges and they repelled each other. The glass rods acquired positive charges and they also repelled each other. But the negatively-charged ebonite rod and the positively-charged glass rod attracted each other. From this we can conclude:

- Like charges repel each other.
- Unlike charges attract each other.

What will happen when a charged object (negative or positive) is brought close to an uncharged object? An uncharged object will always get attracted to a charged object, irrespective of the charge on the body, that is, positive or negative. This shows that from the property of attraction it is difficult to say which of the two objects is charged. Hence, repulsion is a sure test for indicating charges on an object.

- If the object to be tested for charge is attracted by both positively charged objects and negatively charged objects, then the object is said to be neutral or uncharged.
- If the object to be tested for charge is repelled by a positively charged object then the object is said to be positively charged.
- If the object to be tested for charge is repelled by a negatively charged object then the object is said to be negatively charged.

Conservation of Charges

During frictional charging process, the charges transfer the electrons between two objects.

- Charge of an isolated system is conserved.
- Charge can neither be created nor be destroyed but can be transferred from one body to another.

Charging of an Object

Any uncharged object can be charged by using either of the three methods: Charging by friction, charging by conduction or charging by induction.

Charging by Friction

From the previous two activities, we can see that some objects can be charged by rubbing them against another object. When two objects are rubbed together, some electrons from one object get transferred to the other object and the objects become charged. This method of charging an object by rubbing the object with another object is called **charging by friction**.

When a glass rod is rubbed with silk, electrons are transferred from the glass to the silk cloth. This way, the glass rod acquires positive charge and the silk cloth gains electrons, so it acquires negative charge. When an ebonite rod is rubbed with wool/fur, the wool/fur loses electrons, which are transferred to the ebonite rod. This way, the wool acquires positive charge and the ebonite rod becomes negatively charged. Let us do some activities to understand charging by friction.

Activity 3

Aim: To see if various uncharged objects can be charged by rubbing

Materials required: Balloon, eraser, glass rod, plastic ruler, woollen cloth, silk cloth, polythene bag and dry hair

Procedure and observation: Charge the objects by rubbing with the materials as given in the following table and record your observations.

Object	Rub with	Charged/Uncharged
Balloon	Polythene bag/dry hair/ wool/silk	
Eraser	Wool	
Plastic ruler	Dry hair/wool	
Glass rod	Silk	

Activity 4

Aim: To understand charging by friction

Materials required: Ebonite rod, ball of wool and bits of paper

Procedure:

1. Keep the bits of paper on the table.
2. Bring the ebonite rod close to the bits of paper on the table. See what happens.
3. Now, rub the ebonite rod with wool.
4. Again, bring the ebonite rod close to the bits of paper. Observe what happens.

Observation:

Scenario	Outcome
Ebonite rod brought close to the bits of paper	
Ebonite rod rubbed with wool brought close to the bits of paper	

Conclusion: Initially, the ebonite rod is uncharged and hence, does not attract the bits of paper. The ebonite rod gets charged after being rubbed with wool and hence, attracts the bits of paper. The ebonite rod acquires negative charge and the wool acquires an equal amount of positive charge.

Charging by Conduction

When an uncharged object is brought in contact with a charged object, charges flow from the charged object to the uncharged object because every charged object has the tendency to distribute its extra charges to other objects that it comes in contact with. This causes the uncharged object to acquire some charge. This method of charging an object by bringing an uncharged object in contact with a charged object is called **charging by conduction**. During conduction, the type of charge that the uncharged object acquires is the same as that of the charged object.

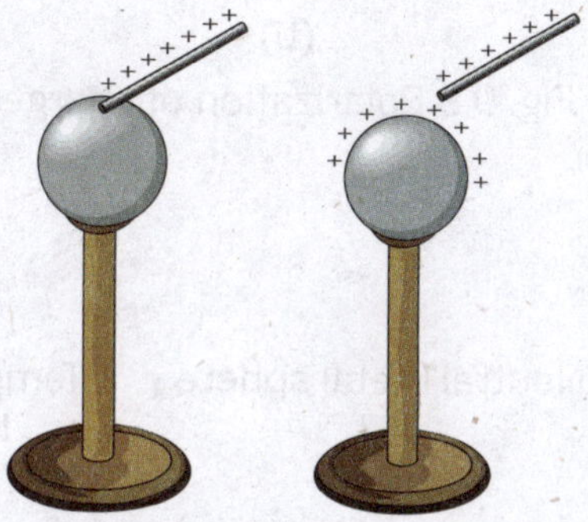

▲ Fig. 9.8 Charging by conduction

For example, when a positively charged glass rod is brought in contact with an uncharged metal sphere, the metal sphere acquires positive charges.

Transfer of Charge

The transfer of charges or the redistribution of charges is always due to the movement of electrons. While additional negative charges (excess of electrons) get distributed by the movement of electrons itself, additional positive charges (deficiency of electrons) attract electrons from elsewhere, thus, creating positive charges wherever the electrons have come from.

Charging by Induction

If a charged object is brought near (but not in contact with) an uncharged object, it acquires a charge opposite to that of the charged object. This method of charging an object by bringing it near a charged object is called **charging by induction**. During induction, the uncharged object acquires the opposite charge. This happens due to a process called polarization of charges. **Polarization** is the separation of positive and negative charges in an object. The process of polarization is as follows:

1. When a negatively-charged object is brought near an uncharged object, the negative charges in both the objects repel each other and the negative charges in the uncharged object move away to the opposite end. So, both ends of the object are charged [Fig. 9.9 (a)].

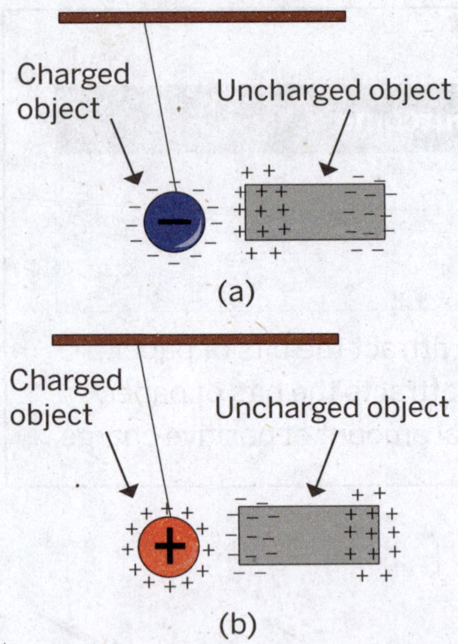

▲ Fig. 9.9 Polarization of charges

2. When a positively-charged object is brought near an uncharged object, the positive charges in the charged object attract the electrons in the uncharged object and the electrons move towards the end near the charged object [Fig. 9.9 (b)].
3. The end of the uncharged object at which the charged object is brought close to is charged opposite to that of the charged object. If the charges at the other end can be removed by **earthing** (creating a path for the charges to flow between the charged object and the earth), the uncharged object attains a charge opposite to the charged object brought in its vicinity.

For example, when a positively charged rod is brought near an uncharged metal sphere, the metal sphere acquires negative charge at the end of the rod and positive charge at the opposite end. These positive charges are removed by earthing thus, making the sphere negatively charged as shown in Fig. 9.10.

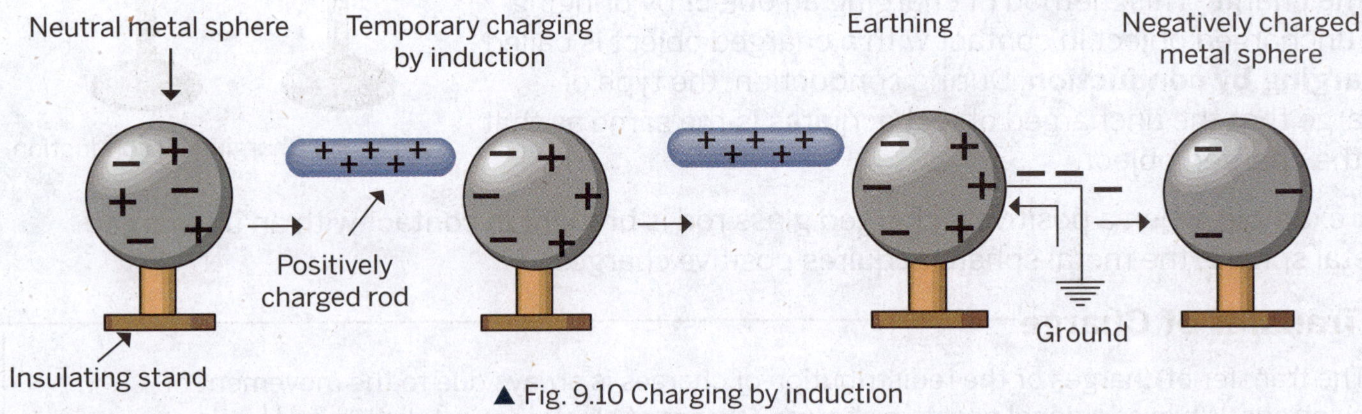

▲ Fig. 9.10 Charging by induction

Electric Discharge

All objects want to be stable or neutral in charge. So, when excess charge builds up on a body, it finds ways to release the excess charge from itself. This process of discarding charge is called **discharge**. Discharge takes place when the charged object is in contact with a conductor. This discharge or flow of extra charges through a conductor produces electric current. The human body is a good conductor.

Science in Context

The human body is a good conductor of electricity. When we touch a charged material, the excess electrons flow between our hand and the conductor. This discharge through our body is the reason behind electric shocks.

How to Reduce Static Electricity?

We experience the effects of static electricity in winter. In winter, the air is dry and charge can easily build up on objects. When the air is humid, that is, when there are water molecules in the air, the charges do not stay long on an object. This is because water molecules have the ability to dissipate excess electrons. So, water is a good remedy for static electricity.

Detection of Charge Using an Electroscope

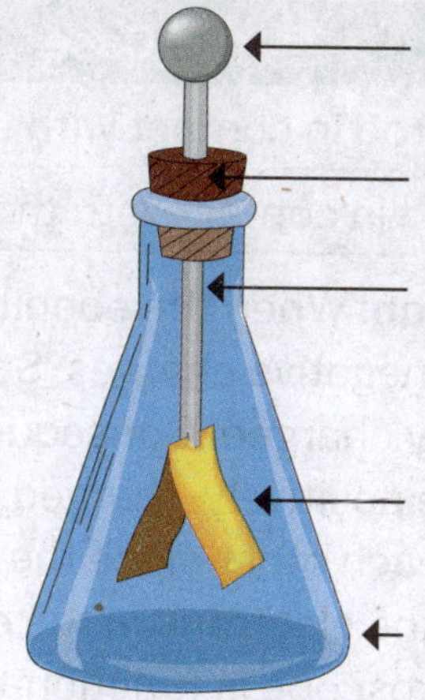

▲ Fig. 9.11 Gold-leaf electroscope

Charge on an object can be detected using a device called **electroscope**. Different types of electroscopes like pith ball electroscope and gold-leaf electroscope are used to detect and measure charges.

In 1787, British physicist Abraham Bennet developed the gold-leaf electroscope. It consists of a thick metallic rod kept vertically and a metallic disc or a sphere connected at one end. Two parallel thin and flexible strips of gold (gold leaves) are hung from the bottom end of the rod. To avoid the effect of wind or air, the gold leaves are enclosed in a glass bottle.

When a negatively charged object is brought close to the metallic sphere, the positive and negative charges in the electroscope will separate due to induction. The metal sphere will be positively charged as the negative charges move towards the leaves due to repulsion. Due to the acquisition of similar charges in the leaves, they will diverge due to repulsion of like charges. The angle through which the gold leaves diverge gives an approximate measure of the charge. The more the amount of charge, the more is the divergence.

Activity 5

Aim: To make a simple electroscope

Materials required: Aluminium foil, thin metal rod, rubber cork, transparent jar with lid, ebonite rod, wool, glass rod and silk

Procedure:

1. Take the thin metal rod and bend its one end to 90°. Fold a 6 cm aluminium strip at the centre and hang it over the bent portion of the thin metal rod as shown in the figure. Insert the other end of the metal rod into the rubber cork, such that there is a 3 cm length projected out.
2. Make a hole in the lid of the jar of the same size as the rubber cork.
3. Fit the rubber cork in the lid along with the setup such that the bent portion of the metal rod with aluminium strip is inside the transparent jar and the 3 cm projection of the metal rod is outside the jar. Make a ball out of the aluminium foil and fix it on the open end of the metal rod.
4. Rub the ebonite rod with wool so that it becomes negatively charged. Now, bring the negatively-charged rod in contact with the metallic sphere of the electroscope. The electroscope gets negatively charged through conduction. Observe the leaf of the electroscope.
5. Rub a glass rod with silk so that it becomes positively charged. Now, bring the glass rod in contact with the metallic sphere of the electroscope. Observe the leaf of the electroscope.

Observation:

Case	Observation
Ebonite rod in contact with the metallic sphere	Leaves move away from each other
Glass rod in contact with the metallic sphere	Leaves move close to each other

Conclusion: When the ebonite rod is brought in contact with the metallic sphere, the sphere acquires negative charges. Some of these charges are transferred to the leaves making them negatively charged. Consequently, the leaves of the electroscope move away from each other. When the positively-charged glass rod is brought in contact with the sphere, the leaves move close to each other since the amount of negative charge in the leaves is reduced. This is because some of the electrons in the electroscope flow to the positively-charged glass rod. That is how, the electroscope is functional.

Activity 6

Aim: To find out the nature of charge present in an object using a gold-leaf electroscope

Materials required: Negatively-charged gold-leaf electroscope and an object with unknown charge

Procedure: Bring the object with unknown charge close to the metallic sphere of the electroscope. Observe the leaves.

Observation: With the metallic sphere of electroscope negatively charged, initially the leaves diverge at an angle. When the object with unknown charge is brought close to the sphere, the two leaves of the electroscope will either move closer or further apart.

Conclusion: If the object is positively charged, the leaves will come closer since the amount of electrons in the leaves will reduce as the object attracts some electrons towards it. If the object is negatively charged, the leaves will move further apart since the amount of electrons in the leaves will increase as the object repels some electrons from the sphere towards the leaves.

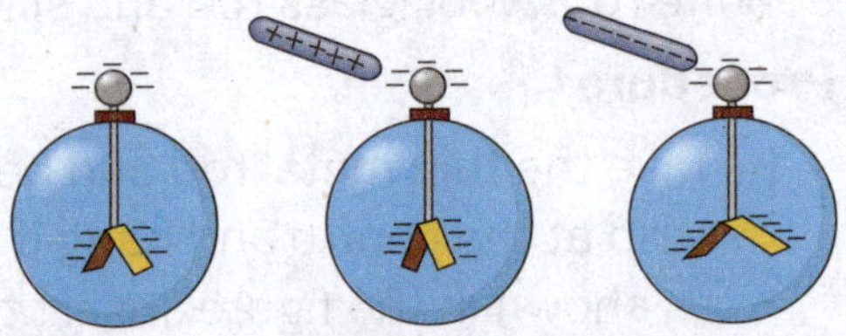

Revision Zone

Fill in the blanks.

1. The leaf of the electroscope will move closer if the charge on the object held close to the metallic sphere is ______________ (opposite/same as) that of the electroscope.
2. Like charges ______________ (attract/repel) each other.
3. In charging by ______________ (friction/conduction), the object to be charged is rubbed with another object.
4. All uncharged objects will have ______________ (equal/unequal) number of electrons and protons.

Lightning

If the accumulation of electrons is very high, the release of electrons or discharge can cause damage to property and life. An example is lightning. **Lightning** is the result of accumulation of static charge in clouds. The powerful discharge of these electric charges among clouds or between clouds and the earth is lightning.

This static charging of the clouds is believed to be due to frictional charging. Clouds contain millions of water particles suspended in them. Water evaporates from Earth's surface and rises up. Upon cooling, it forms droplets and several droplets combine to form clouds. The droplets moving upwards collide with the water droplets already suspended in the cloud. During these collisions, electrons are ripped off from the rising droplets causing the bottom of the clouds to become negatively charged. The positively-charged droplets rise up to the top of the clouds making the region positively charged. This results in the polarization of charges in the clouds. That is, the top region of the clouds becomes positively charged and the bottom region becomes negatively charged.

As more and more charge builds up in the clouds, an increased electric field is created around the clouds in the atmosphere, which makes the atmosphere highly conductive. This makes way for an easy path for the transfer of charges from the clouds to the surface of Earth. Huge amounts of light and heat are produced in the air during this discharge. This is what we see as lightning in the sky. Lightning is accompanied by a loud sound called **thunder** that we hear after lightning. This is because light travels faster than sound and so, we see lightning first and then hear thunder.

▲ Fig. 9.12 Lightning

Know the Scientist

American scientist **Benjamin Franklin** (1706–1790) explained the phenomenon of lightning in the 18th century. He flew a kite during a thunderstorm and collected the electric charges in a Leyden jar (a device used to store electric charges) every time the kite was struck by lightning. This led him to suggest that lightning is an electrical phenomenon. He also invented the lightning conductor.

Science in Context

Earth's atmosphere contains lots of dust particles and other impurities. So, the transfer of charges (discharge) from the clouds to Earth's surface does not happen in a straight line because of the floating dust particles. This is the reason behind the zig-zag branching in lightning bolts. Also, the purplish glow of lightning is a characteristic of ionized air molecules.

Types and Effects of Lightning

Lightning is mainly of three types. The first type is the lightning that takes place within the same cloud. The second type is the lightning that takes place between two clouds. The third type of lightning takes place between clouds and Earth.

Do You Know?

The study of lightning is called fulminology.

When a lightning bolt between a cloud and Earth hits an object like tall buildings and trees on Earth, it is called a **lightning strike**. A lightning strike can destroy trees, buildings, etc., completely. In hilly areas, the chances of lightning strike are more than in valleys because the distance between hill tops and clouds is lesser than the distance between valleys and clouds.

Though lightning causes a lot of damage, it is also beneficial in some ways. During lightning, the heat and light produced enhances the combination of atmospheric nitrogen with oxygen to form oxides of nitrogen. These oxides of nitrogen dissolve in rainwater and come down as very dilute nitric acid, which reacts with different salts and minerals present in the soil to form nitrogenous compounds. These nitrogenous compounds are required for the growth of plants.

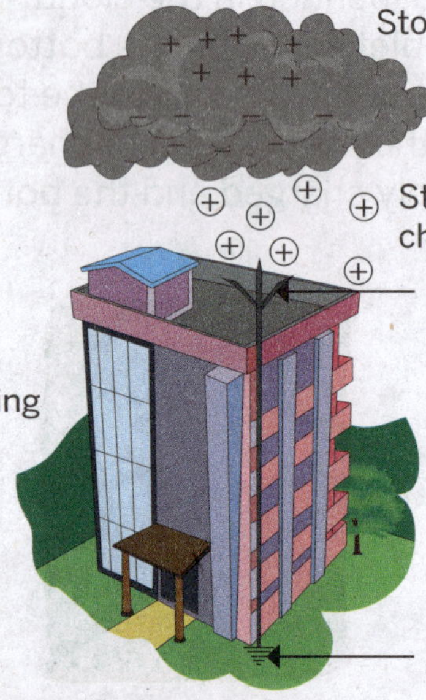

▲ Fig. 9.13 Lightning conductor

Lightning Conductor

Lightning conductor is a device that helps to protect tall buildings, monuments and towers from damage due to lightning. Lightning conductor is made up of a thick metal rod with spikes at the top. The spiked end is fixed on the top of the building and the rod runs down the building. The bottom end of the rod is connected to a copper plate buried deep under the earth.

A lightning conductor provides a low resistance path to the flow of charges. Therefore, during a lightning strike electric charges flow through the lightning conductor to the earth and not through the building.

Safety and Precautions During a Lightning Storm

- If you are in an open ground, lie down flat on the ground. Stay away from tall objects like trees and electric posts.
- If travelling, do not come out of the vehicle. Staying inside a car is safer than standing in the open.
- Keep away from wired devices like telephone and television.
- If you live in a multistoried house or building, then ensure a lightning conductor is fixed to the building.

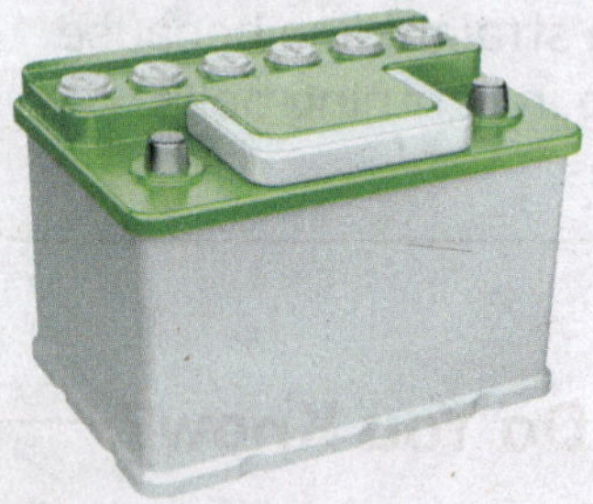
▲ Fig. 9.14 Car battery

Battery

We have learned that a combination of two or more cells is called a **battery**. A single cell is not sufficient to provide electric current for some appliances. So, a number of cells of the same type combined in a series can be used to provide the required potential difference and the current. Lead acid accumulator used in vehicles as a battery is a combination of six cells connected in a series. Batteries are available in different shapes and sizes.

Very small cells are used to power devices like hearing aids and wristwatches. Very big batteries are used to provide standby power in the absence of current from the mains.

Dangers of Electricity

If not handled carefully, working with electricity can be dangerous. It can damage the electrical appliances and circuits. It can cause electric shocks which may even lead to death. Here are the some of the major electrical injuries.

The main types of electrical injuries are:

- Electrical Shock
- Electrical Burns
- Blasts due to pressure impact

Electric shock occurs when the body becomes part of an electrical circuit. Touching the live wire causes electric shock. Following situations increase the chance of electrical shocks.

1. Exposed electrical parts
2. Overloaded circuits
3. Improper grounding or earthing
4. Damaged power lines
5. Wet conditions

Electrical safety and Precautions

1. **Poor wiring and defective electric wires:** Poor wiring can increase chance of fire, power surges, arc faults, and other serious consequences. Damaged, worn, cracked or corroded electrical wires can increase the chance of electrical accidents.
2. **Outlets close to water:** Outlets in bathrooms, kitchens, and other living areas with water should be installed at a fair distance from the water source. As water conducts electricity, keeping outlets away from water reduces the chance of electric shock. Never use a radio, hair dryer, phone, or other device in the bath, near the pool, or anywhere with a wet floor.
3. **Wet hands:** Electrical appliances should never be handled with wet hands as this heightens the chance of getting an electric shock. Keep appliances far away from sinks, bathtubs, showers, and taps.
4. **Pouring water on electrical fires:** A common error people do is pouring water on electrical fires. If an electrical fire occurs, avoid pouring water on the flames as water will further fuel the fire and could cause electrocution. Keep a fire extinguisher on site if you're worried about electrical fires and use that instead of water in times of emergency. If you don't have one nearby, turn off your electrical power, evacuate your home and call the fire brigade.
5. **Inquisitive young children:** Any electrical outlet at their height and within their reach can be replaced with EXTRA-SAFE power points. These can be interchanged with normal power point and prevent sharp objects and fingers from going into the socket. Unprotected sockets can lead to serious injury.

6. **Electric lamp:** Incandescent lamps like all sources of electricity, can also cause electric shock, so ensure you always turn the light switch OFF before replacing an incandescent lamp, and never replace lamp or touch a lamp switch with wet hands. Always ensure you use an incandescent lamp with the correct wattage to prevent overheating.
7. Make sure that items like computer and television have enough space around them for ventilation, to prevent them from overheating.
8. Never try to repair electrical appliances yourself, always contact a licensed electrician.
9. Check your appliances regularly for faulty switches, plugs and frayed cords.
10. Avoid overloading power board with too many appliances at once. For example, if you have a heater plugged into the power board, unplug it before using the hair dryer.
11. Never poke anything into an appliance while it is plugged in or in use.
12. Always use outdoor grade extension cord outside the house.
13. Make sure your hands are dry before touching switches or electrical appliances.
14. Before cleaning areas like the kitchen, bathroom or laundry, make sure all appliances are switched OFF.
15. Do not remove the plug from the outlet point by pulling the cord, pull the plug to remove it.
16. Always use safety device like an electric fuse or MCB to protect the circuit and the electrical appliances, and make sure that they are not defective.
17. Do not handle electrical appliances with bare feet. It may cause electric shocks in case of any short circuit.
18. Always switch OFF the main switch of your house before carrying out any electrical repairs.
19. Always make sure that the electrical appliances are of the approved standards. Always keep them away from water. Since, water is a good conductor of electricity, water entering into the appliances may cause short circuit.
20. Always wear rubber sandals while handling any electrical appliance.

Revision Zone

Fill in the blanks.

1. Lightning is the result of accumulation of ____________ (static charge/electricity) in clouds.
2. The bottom of a lightning conductor is connected to a ____________ (conductor/insulator).
3. Accumulation of static charge in clouds results in ____________ (lightning/thunder).

Keywords

Cation: a positively-charged ion

Anion: a negatively-charged ion

Polarization: separation of positive and negative charges

Discharge: the process of discarding charge

Lightning: the powerful discharge of electric charges that develop in clouds

In a Nutshell

- Any object that loses electrons or gains electrons will become a charged object.
- Charging of an object can be done by the method of friction, conduction and induction.
- Power: energy used or consumed per unit of time
- Electroscope is a device that can help in detecting the charges on an object.
- Electric fuse and MCB are the safety devices that protect electric circuits from excess current.
- Lightning: A flash of light produced due to the electric discharge between the clouds and the Earth

Exercise

1 Choose the correct answer for each of the following.

a. All uncharged objects will have
   i. more electrons
   ii. more protons
   iii. equal number of protons and electrons
   iv. equal number of protons and neutrons

b. An object can be charged by the method of
   i. friction only   ii. conduction only
   iii. induction only   iv. All of the above

c. The leaves of a charged electroscope will move apart if the object in contact has
   i. same charge as the electroscope
   ii. opposite charge as the electroscope
   iii. neutral charge
   iv. charge of any nature

d. When a cloud gets charged
   i. the top region of the cloud is negatively charged and the bottom region is positively charged
   ii. the top region of the cloud is positively charged and the bottom region is negatively charged
   iii. the top and the bottom regions of the cloud are positively charged
   iv. the top and the bottom regions of the cloud are negatively charged

e. The device that helps in detecting charge on an object is
   i. electroscope   ii. lightning conductor
   iii. ammeter   iv. voltmeter

f. Kilowatt-hour is the unit of
   i. electric energy
   ii. electric power
   iii. electric charge
   iv. electric current

g. Which among the following is used as a safety device to protect electric circuits?
   i. Electric iron
   ii. Electric fuse
   iii. Electric meter
   iv. Electric bulb

h. Which of the following is the most appropriate for the phenomenon of lightning?
   i. Lightning is caused due to an electric discharge between the clouds only.
   ii. Lightning is caused due to an electric discharge between the clouds and the Earth only.
   iii. Lightning is caused due to an electric discharge between the clouds and between clouds and the Earth.
   iv. Lightning is not caused by electric discharge between clouds.

2 Write T for True and F for False.

a. Like charges repel each other.
b. Lightning is a discharge of electric charges between clouds and Earth.
c. The direction of flow of conventional current is in the direction of flow of electrons.
d. We should keep away from wired devices during lightning.

e. Commercially, electrical energy is measured in joules.

f. The SI unit of electrical energy is kilowatt-hour.

g. It is safe to handle electrical appliances with wet hands.

h. Staying inside a house or a building is safe at the time of lightning.

3 Fill in the blanks.

a. Charging by conduction is possible only in the case of __________ (conductors/insulators).

b. Charging of objects by rubbing is possible only by __________ (induction/friction) method.

c. The thick metal rod with spikes fixed at the top of buildings is called a __________ (lightning conductor/electroscope).

d. The gold-leaf electroscope was developed by __________ (Benjamin Franklin/Abraham Bennet).

e. The process of connecting a charged object to the Earth is called __________. (earthing/conduction)

4 Match the following.

a. Charging by rubbing	i. Lightning conductor
b. Charging by contact	ii. Induction
c. Charging by distance	iii. Electroscope
d. Charge detector	iv. Conduction
e. Device with spikes	v. Friction

5 Define the following.

a. Conductor

b. Earth wire

c. Static electricity

d. Electric Power

e. Lightning

6 Differentiate between the following.

a. Protons and electrons

b. Cation and anion

c. Free electrons and bound electrons

d. Charging by conduction and charging by induction

e. Lightning and thunder

7 Name the following.

a. Imbalance of electric charge between two bodies due to the build-up of charges on a body.

b. Objects that allow free flow of charges on them.

c. The powerful discharge of electric charges acquired by a cloud.

d. The charge acquired by a body when it loses one electron.

e. A test for presence of charge on a body.

f. The safety device used to protect the electrical appliances and circuits.

g. A device specially designed and used to protect tall buildings from lightning.

8 Answer the following questions in brief.

a. What is a lightning strike?

b. Why thunder is always heard after lightning?

c. What are the three types of lightning?

d. Name the particles which constitute an atom.

e. What is an atom?

f. What causes lightning?

g. Mention any two safety measures to be taken while handling electricity.

h. Explain the role of a fuse.

i. What is a miniature circuit breaker?

9 Answer the following questions in detail.

a. Explain the advantages and disadvantages of lightning. What are the precautions to be taken during a lightning strike?
b. Explain the different methods of charging a body.
c. What is a lightning conductor and how does it help in saving a building from lightning strikes?
d. What is an electroscope and how does it function? Explain with a labelled diagram.
e. List the safety measures that should be taken while handling electricity.
f. John uses an electric iron of 1000 W for 30 minutes a day, a geyser of 2000 W for one hour a day and 7 bulbs of power 100 W for 3 hours a day. The reading of his electricity meter on 1 June 2016 was 3310. What will be the reading at the end of the month. Also, calculate the amount to be paid if the rate of one unit is ₹4.
g. Like charges repel each other and unlike charges attract each other. Explain this phenomenon with the help of an activity.

10 Think and answer.

a. There is a pine tree, a man and an elephant in an open ground. Which one of them will be hit first in case of a lightning strike?
b. What is the charge on the gold leaf in the electroscope shown below?

11 Project

Making a simple electroscope:

You can make a simple improvised electroscope at home and detect the charges on objects.

Materials required: Glass bottle, a rectangular piece of cardboard, paperclip, thin aluminium foil

Procedure: Open one end of a paperclip and insert the other end through the centre of cardboard. Take a small rectangular piece of thin aluminium foil of dimensions 4 cm × 1 cm.

Fold the aluminium foil in the middle and hang it on the hook of paperclip along the fold. Now, insert the paperclip along with the aluminium foil on it into the bottle so that the cardboard rests on the mouth of the bottle. Make a small ball of aluminium foil and fix it on the other end of the paperclip outside the bottle. Now, bring a charged ebonite rod near the aluminium foil ball. You can see that the two leaves of the aluminium foil hung on the copper wire move apart. This indicates that the ebonite rod is a charged object.

12 In the Library

Van de Graff generator is a device that can develop voltages of more than 10,000 volts by continuous charging. Read more about the Van de Graff generator, its construction and working.

Worksheet

Subject Integration

1. A sphere containing equal number of positive and negative charges (neutral sphere) is given below. What will happen when a positively charged rod is brought near it?

   Explain it diagrammatically in the space provided below.

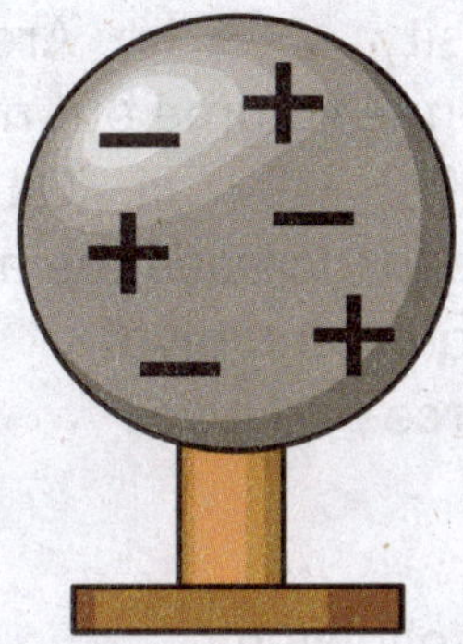

2. Keep your electricity bill in your hand. Suppose the unit reading in electric meter is 150 units. The first 30 units are charged as ₹3 per unit. The next 70 units are charged as ₹4.50. The rest units are charged as ₹6. Calculate the electric bill for 150 units. Mention the SI unit of electrical energy.

Assessments

Assessment 1 (Chapters 1-4)

Maximum: 40

1 Choose the correct answer for each of the following. (5 × 1 = 5)

a. Solids cannot be compressed and stored because the ______
   i. molecules are very loosely packed
   ii. molecules are tightly packed
   iii. intermolecular force is weak
   iv. all of the above

b. Volume of a substance can be calculated using the following formula.
   i. Mass/Area
   ii. Area/ Density
   iii. Area/Mass
   iv. Mass/ Density

c. Which of the following has a definite volume but not a definite shape?
   i. Book
   ii. Stone
   iii. Oil
   iv. Table

d. Which of the following changes can increase the moment of force on an object?
   i. Increase distance between force and pivot
   ii. Reduce distance between force and pivot
   iii. Reduce magnitude of force
   iv. Remove the pivot

e. The flowing river possesses the following
   i. kinetic energy
   ii. gravitational potential energy
   iii. elastic potential energy
   iv. potential energy

2 Fill in the blanks. (5 × 1 = 5)

a. Melting is otherwise termed as ______. (fusion/fission)

b. Density of irregular solid can be measured using ______. (Conical flask/Eureka can)

c. The term atmospheric pressure represents the pressure exerted by ______ .(liquids/gases)

d. A door opening around a fixed hinge is an example of ______.(moment/pressure)

e. One newton metre is equal to one ______ (joule/watt)

3 Write T for True and F for False. (5 × 1 = 5)

a. Intermolecular force is very strong in gases.

b. Density of a substance can be determined by knowing area and volume.

c. The SI unit of force is newton metre (Nm).

d. Stretched spring is an example for elastic potential energy.

e. A point about which an object can turn is called pivot.

4 Give reasons for the following. (5 × 2 = 10)

a. Solids are hard and rigid

b. Camel walks easily in desert.

c. Pressure increases with the decrease in the volume.

d. Wood floats on water while nail sinks.

e. Thrill while riding in roller coaster.

5 Answer the following questions. (5 × 3 = 15)

a. Differentiate between condensation and sublimation.

b. List any two examples of substances that float on water.

c. List any two applications of pressure.

d. What are the two factors that moment depends on?

e. Derive the relation between work and energy.

Assessment 2 (Chapters 5-9)

Maximum: 40

1 Choose the correct answer for each of the following. (5 × 1 = 5)

a. The phenomenon of bending of light rays is called

i. reflection ii. refraction iii. lateral shift iv. dispersion

b. Which mirror is used as the rear view mirror of vehicles?

i. Plane mirror ii. Concave mirror iii. Cylindrical mirror iv. Convex mirror

c. The tendency of matter to expand in its length is called __________ .

i. linear expansion ii. superficial expansion
iii. volume expansion iv. cubical expansion.

d. Sound can easily travel through __________ .

i. vacuum ii. solids iii. liquids iv. gases

e. Combination of two or more cells is called __________ .

i. resistor ii. battery iii. switch iv. fuse

2 Fill in the blanks. (5 × 1 = 5)

a. A mirror whose reflecting surface is on the outer side is called __________ (convex/concave) mirror.

b. Frequency is measured using __________ (decibel/hertz)

c. Hot air balloon rises in the sky due to thermal expansion of __________. (gases/liquids)

d. The device used to protect electric circuit is __________. (fuse/battery)

e. The commercial unit of electrical energy is __________ (kilowatt-hour/watt)

3 Write T for True and F for False. (5 × 1 = 5)

a. Plane mirror always produces a real image.

b. Concave mirror always produce enlarged image.

c. Vapourization can occur through melting.

d. All charged objects will have equal number of electrons and protons

e. An electroscope can be used to test the nature of charge on a body.

4 Give reasons for the following. (5 × 2 = 10)

a. Convex mirror does not form real images.

b. Female voice is shriller than male voice.

c. A hot object gets cold after some time.

d. We hear thunder after seeing lightning.

e. When a scale is rubbed on hair and brought close to the bits of paper, it gets attracted.

5 Answer the following questions. (5 × 3 = 15)

a. Write any two differences between real image and virtual image.

b. Explain the cause of dispersion of light.

c. Write the relation between pitch and frequency

d. What is thermal expansion? Given an example of thermal expansion of solid.

e. Explain the role of a fuse in an electric circuit.

Things to Remember

Important Formulae	
1. Density, $D = \frac{m}{V}$ 2. Moment = Force × distance arm 3. Pressure = $\frac{\text{Force}}{\text{Area}}$ 4. Weight, $W = mg$ 5. Fluid pressure at the bottom of the container, $P = h\,\rho\,g$ 6. The apparent weight of the body in water, $W_{apparent} = W - W_b$	7. Work done = Force x Displacement 8. Gravitational potential energy = $m\,g\,h$ 9. Kinetic energy, $KE = \frac{1}{2}mv^2$ 10. Refractive index, $\mu = \frac{c}{v}$ 11. $\frac{\sin i}{\sin r} = \frac{\mu_2}{\mu_1} = \frac{v_1}{v_2}$ 12. Speed of light in any medium, $v = \frac{\text{Speed of light in vacuum}}{\text{Refractive index of the medium}}$

Physical quantities	Unit	Symbol
Density	kilogram per cubic metre	kg/m^3
Pressure	pascal	Pa
	newton per square metre	N/m^2
Energy	joule	J
	calorie	cal
Frequency	hertz	Hz
Sound	decibel	dB
Charge	coulomb	C
Voltage	joules per coulomb	J/C
	volt	V
Current	ampere	A
Power	watt	W
Electrical energy consumed	kilo-watt hour	kWh